# Uniquely Gifted

*special friend!*
*Stuart Calvert*
*1 Peter 4:10*

# Discovering Your Spiritual Gifts

# Stuart Calvert

Published by:
New Hope
P.O. Box 12065
Birmingham, Alabama 35202-2065

Cover design by Barry Graham

Dewey Decimal Classification: 234.13
Subject Headings:   GIFTS (THEOLOGY)
                    HOLY SPIRIT
                    CHURCH WORK

ISBN: 1-56309-061-9
N934107•0593•5M1

# Contents

# Thank You, Giver of Gifts

The centerpiece resembled a jack-in-the-box of bears—the cuddly stuffed animals anchored bobbing balloons that hovered just below the ceiling. Cupcakes iced with red, blue, and yellow dollops of divinity rested on a pedestal stand. Bears and balloons decorated the neatly arranged plates and napkins. All these decorations served as a festive backdrop for the focal point: a pretty cake inscribed, "Happy Birthday, Sarah."

The honoree sat on the floor, swathed in tissue and ribbon that moments before had concealed her first birthday gifts. When the fancy wrappings revealed a bracelet or a pop-up book, a push toy or spinning top, Sarah's mother would repeat, "Say 'thank you,' Sarah." Mother's futile attempt to teach courtesy cued Sarah to reach her chubby hand for the next bow. Saying "thank you" was unnecessary. The special glee that made her eyes smile and her little body bounce with excitement showed "thank you."

Birthdays! The anniversary of the beginning of life deserves a celebration. Photographs and tucked-away mementos are our only memories of our first birthday. However, other birthdays, celebrated with splendid or simple parties and special presents, have their own memories. I remember a favorite party: lanterns strung through the pine trees, hot dogs with all the trimmings, chocolate cake, and a shiny red bicycle.

The new bike helped me to compete in races up and down Ann Street Hill. The hill was both a playmate and a foe for all the children in the neighborhood. It plagued us with rocks, ruts, and red dust on sunny days, and gooey mud on rainy ones. Staying vertical was a challenge. To conquer the steep hill, I had to gather speed two blocks away. The momentum, aided by strenuous puffing and pumping, propelled the bike over the hill.

Ann Street was the route I rode my bike to Bible school. Everyday Mrs. Rooks impressed us with the meaning of John 3:16: "For God so loved the world, that He gave His only begotten Son, that whosoever believeth in Him should not perish, but have everlasting life" (KJV). Every day the hill loomed higher. Somber thoughts about sin and my need for a Saviour weighed on my heart and sapped my physical strength. Then one noon, as Ann Street Hill came into view, I said, "Yes, Jesus, I love You, too. I'm sorry I'm bad. Forgive me. Save me." In an instant, I was over the top . . . happy, unburdened, free!

What happened at the foot of Ann Street Hill? A child was born again! I trusted God's Word, "For it is by God's grace that you have been saved through faith. It is not the result of your own efforts, but God's gift . . ." (Eph. 2:8-9 TEV). My! What an extravagant, merciful gift: undeserved forgiveness for all my sins and a right standing with God; a binding love relationship that nothing can sever; release from the law and freedom to grow under grace into the likeness of Christ; my own personal place in the body of Christ—the church; the presence of Christ's Spirit within me; eternal life. Each of these mercies to which my child-like "yes" responded is equally significant.

What happened at the foot of Ann Street Hill (and in your special place)? The Holy Spirit quietly entered my life. However, His initial entrance into individual lives was spectacular. After Jesus' ascension, the perplexed disciples waited in Jerusalem for the gift Jesus promised would come from the Father. An international crowd was in the city to celebrate the Feast of Pentecost. Feeling apart from the festivities, these timid believers trembled. Suddenly a rushing wind dramatized the presence of the Holy Spirit. Accompanying the wind, a mass of flames covered the group. Then a single flame of fire settled on each person. The joyous believers, through Spirit-inspired utterances, boldly praised God for His magnificent deeds.

The Holy Spirit energized the believers for service (see Acts 2), empowered Peter to preach (Acts 2:17-21), convinced the lost to repent (Acts 2:37-42), filled the church to make it a living, learning, unified, praying, sharing, worshiping (Acts 2:42-47), and witnessing organism (Acts 1:8).

What happened at the foot of Ann Street Hill? The Holy Spirit transformed a temporary tabernacle of a body into an eternal temple. He caused a clay vessel to pulsate with resurrection power and to shine with the same glory that eliminates the need of a sun in heaven.

Sorting through the flaws of my imperfect life, I see the imprint of His presence and feel the impact of His actions. You do, too. Remember the depressive despair when you could not pray and the Holy Spirit interceded? the fresh insight of a familiar Scripture passage when He taught you? the loneliness before He satisfied your need? the indecision, when He came to guide you? the witnessing opportunity, when He gave you boldness? your rebellion and His grief? your haste and His calming?

What happened at the foot of Ann Street Hill? The Holy Spirit initiated the possibility for me to be like Christ. Paul refers to the Christ-like qualities as fruit of the Spirit (see Gal. 5:22-23). In addition, the Holy Spirit is a person with the qualities described in Isaiah 11:1-2. These characteristics of the King are fulfilled in the person and work of our Lord:

• Wisdom: insight to see the true situation.
• Understanding: ability to make an intelligent decision.
• Counsel: ability to view facts and make right decisions.
• Might: strength to do God's will.
• Knowledge: the know-how to perform a task because of fellowship with God.
• Fear of the Lord: reverence for God.

Notice that these qualities lean strongly toward the intellectual. This is important in a consideration of the Spirit. Often we equate His presence with emotionalism in opposition to practical understanding. The Holy Spirit illuminates our minds as well as our emotions.

Understanding His presence and work is crucial to a study about spiritual gifts.

What happened at the foot of Ann Street Hill? The Holy Spirit brought me a gift. My gift from God, the Holy Spirit, is also a Gift Giver. Always pointing to Jesus, the Holy Spirit gives us gifts that enable us to honor and praise the Lord. He assigned us one or more gifts the day we were born again. He plans for us to use our gifts within a sphere of service.

Eventually Sarah will learn to say "thank you" for birthday presents, though I hope she never loses the smile and the bounce that shows her enthusiastic appreciation. Saying "Thank you, Lord, for saving me" is a daily, sincere expression of gratitude through prayer. Showing my gratitude by ministering through my gift is an enthusiastic way to celebrate the occasion and anniversary of my rebirth.

## I Am Uniquely Gifted

When we moved to our first pastorate, I tried to be all things to all people. I made almost every step my pastor-husband made, except when he stood in the pulpit to preach. Even then I was close behind him in the choir. Now, I appreciate music from classical to country, but I cannot produce a musical sound worth listening to. By sitting in the choir, I satisfied my personal need for the congregation to see me, the preacher's wife, in church.

I scheduled my time so that one day I visited shut-ins; one day, the sick; one day, the prospects; one day, the absentees. I was involved in leadership roles in all the missions organizations, taught an adult Sunday School class, and led a youth Church Training group. When I was not going somewhere, I was preparing for all the doing.

No doubt the feelings came gradually, but one day I suddenly realized I felt wilted and worn out. I discovered that I did not like the shut-ins, the sick, the prospects, the absentees, or Stuart. I was even beginning to look a little skeptically at my husband Bob! I felt certain that if I had to teach any*thing* else to any*body* else, I would start screaming as loud as I could and never stop.

Thank God, when the treadmill of my busyness slowed, I didn't shrug my shoulders and say, "This is my lot in life." I didn't grit my teeth and try to continue living my self-imposed role. When the treadmill slowed, I let the Lord lift me off.

First, I took a long look at *self*. Buried beneath what I assumed to be expectations of so many people, I found that I did not know who I was. At that point I promised to keep in touch with *me*. Keeping that promise became a continuing, life-long process.

Second, I changed. I turned loose of some activities. The choir went first. Someone was waiting and willing to teach the adult Sunday School class. To my surprise the church did not disenfranchise me! I continued to lead one youth missions organization and the youth group. I concentrated on loving the young people, and on developing my ability to work with them.

A good rapport with the girls enabled me to befriend their families and be welcomed in their homes. One day I answered my phone to hear a distraught mother sob, "Come help us. Beth is pregnant." The thought of an unwed, thirteen year old child becoming a mother stunned me. On that day I entered Beth's life with a timid reluctance, and the Holy Spirit began to teach me about acceptance, empathy, and listening. The moment Beth and I said "hello," I liked her exactly as she was.

At some point during her pregnancy, I realized I could participate with ease in the lives of people in crises. When I stepped off the treadmill of over involvement, the Lord revealed a gift He had placed in me—the gift of mercy. One immediate result was that the days of my week changed from bondage to an activity-hopping calendar, to experiencing an Emmaus walk—touching, caring, listening, and loving as I walked with my Saviour.

The Lord continued to enhance and expand the gift of mercy in me. I became a Volunteer in Probation with the juvenile court. The experiences with my delinquent friends initiated invitations for me to write and speak. The gift thrust me into a variety of opportunities that I call "spiritual spinoffs." Each new venture is a direct or indirect result of the gift of mercy.

Proverbs 18:16 promises that "a gift opens the way for the giver and ushers him into the presence of the great" (NIV). Wherever you are in the Lord's body, your gift gives you a place to serve. True, we may never hear the world applaud our gifts. More important, however, we will hear the most rewarding accolade, "Well done, good and faithful servant" (Matt. 25:23a NIV).

## You Are Uniquely Gifted

In preparation for this study I asked women, "What is your spiritual gift?" Most of the responses were questions:

"Did you say *fruit* or *gifts*? Are they the same?"

"Do you mean my talent?"

"Do I have one?" Making a distinction between gifts, fruit, and talents will be a starting point for our study of spiritual gifts.

Lend me your imagination. When the apostle Paul walked the streets of Corinth, Rome, and Ephesus, daily news sheets, posted on prominent columns or *graffito* walls, informed the public of proclamations, local news, and announcements. When a courier shouted, "Hear Ye, Hear Ye," citizens gathered to read or hear the day's edicts. In your imagination, place yourself in Paul's setting; follow the crowd to the news column.

# Hear Ye, Hear Ye!
# Spiritual Gifts Differ From the Fruit
# of the Spirit!

| GIFTS | FRUIT |
|---|---|
| Abilities given for service | Qualities of Christlike character: love, joy, peace, patience, kindness, goodness, faithfulness, humility, self-control |
| Defines what a Christian does | Defines who a Christian is |
| Christ's ministry through us | Christ's qualities in us |
| Discovered with the help of the Holy Spirit | Developed by the Holy Spirit with our cooperation |
| Temporary use on earth | Eternal quality in earth and heaven |
| Distributed among believers (one teaches, another helps) | All fruit represented in every believer |
| Primary purpose: To strengthen believers; to edify the church | Primary purpose: To enable believers to grow and mature in Christlikeness |

Every time Paul began a new church, he helped the believers understand their spiritual gifts. Within each "gift" passage, he also described how the fruit of the Spirit affects the use of the gifts. Spiritual gifts equip Christians to minister, doing God's work in the world. The fruit of the Spirit enables Christians to express the attitudes and to live the behavior that should accompany ministry in Jesus' name. The fruit is the medium through which the gifts are expressed.

## Hear Ye, Hear Ye!
## Spiritual Gifts Differ From Talents!

| GIFTS | TALENTS |
|---|---|
| Given by God, our Redeemer, at conversion | Given by God, our Creator, at natural birth |
| Possessed only by Christians | Possessed by Christians and non-Christians |
| Developed by the power of the Holy Spirit Who uses human methods at times | Developed by human training |
| Divine endowment | Natural ability |
| Purpose: Christian service | Purpose: instruct, entertain, inspire |

God may use human means to reveal and strengthen gifts that are given by the Spirit. The Holy Spirit nudged me toward the court. Then the court trained me to work with delinquents.

A consecrated talent can become a channel through which a gift is exercised. With a pinch of this and a dash of that, a talented cook can prepare tasty meals served simply or with a flair. Her gift may be hospitality or help. Cooking becomes a channel to use that gift. A talented singer with the gift of evangelism can lead lost people to Jesus through the message in music. A talented artist with the gift of teaching can help others understand God's message through visuals, paintings, or chalk talks.

Mae's talent is quilting. Her gifts are evangelism, exhortation, and encouragement. At flea markets, she sells quilts and shares her faith by telling others what Jesus means to her and handing out tracts. Her sweet attitude and words of hope cheer the disheartened.

## Hear Ye, Hear Ye!
## Yes, You Are Gifted!
## New Testament Churches, Filled With Gifted People, Tell You So!

Mr. Flora, a deacon in our first church, enthusiastically welcomed us, saying, "Our little church is filled with all kinds of folks. You'll like us!" Mr. Flora stated a truth I have observed in each of our pastorates: all kinds of folks do fill the church. The significance of that truth is not in the distinctive personalities of church members. God plans to work through the individuals He has gifted in distinctive ways.

All kinds of folks have formed the church since its beginning. Some who lived in Corinth heard the gospel, repented, and became a part of the body of Christ—the church. Still clinging to Corinthian ethics, they were greedy, gluttonous, and factious. Without a pattern to follow, they formed a church.

Several hundred miles away, in Rome, lived a people obsessed with power, patriotism, and gory sports events. The citizens and slaves lived in a spiritual void. Some of these Romans heard the gospel. They repented and shared the message, "Jesus the Messiah is Lord" to a populace that shouted, "Caesar is Lord." Without a pattern to follow, they formed a church.

Out in the back country, the city of Ephesus lay like a sprawling cancer. Every vice imaginable lured tourists to the city. Abandoning themselves to vile conduct, the residents and tourists lost their sense of shame and decency. When Paul preached, many responded to the gospel. As they shared their new faith, they changed the society of their city. Without a pattern to follow, they formed a church.

Up in the pioneer area of Asia Minor persecuted

Christians struggled. Peter encouraged them to live as people who belong to Christ. Without a pattern to follow, they formed churches.

How could new believers from pagan backgrounds form churches? God generously gave those first Christians every necessary spiritual gift for ministering and witnessing in a decadent society. He gave every necessary resource to build a church in a pagan culture. With complete dependence on the Holy Spirit, the first century Christians turned the world upside down.

The churches begun by Paul and Peter will be the points of reference for our study. I invite you to meander along on our imaginary walk through the cities and into the churches.

## Hear Ye, Hear Ye!
## Thoughts to Mull Along the Way

• How much energy do our churches expend on planning exciting programs to attract people? Do we assess the needs then discern which gifted members can satisfy the needs? Do we appreciate the benefit we receive from gifted folks outside our local church? Gifts from others reach us in the form of innumerable resources, from products to people. However, resources must be the servants of the gifts.

• Are we suspicious of any spontaneous activity of the Holy Spirit that interrupts rigid agendas? Can we explain all of our busyness in human terms? Is everything we do the result of human effort? Is it possible to become too programmed?

• Do we stress the discovery of gifts rather than filling positions in the church organization? Do we trust the Holy Spirit to call members to ministries? In one church, a woman became concerned about four young people handicapped by mental retardation. In each situation, family members rotated staying at home on Sunday with the handicapped child or sibling. The woman felt compelled to help. With no formal instruction in special education, she read books and attended seminars to learn about the needs of special people. Then in a room equipped with material resources designed for the mentally retarded, the teacher welcomed four new members to Sunday School. Her class attendance was one hundred percent every Sunday. In addition, four other family members were now able to attend church regularly. A silent call from the Holy Spirit was heard and heeded by a gifted teacher.

• After moving to a new area, do we search for a church with the best choir or youth program, the most popular pastor, or fully equipped family life center? Or do we search for a church lacking in the gift we can offer?

Researching spiritual gifts revolutionized my understanding of what the church should be and do in the world. I was thrilled to observe how God's Spirit directly led the early Christians. Could my church depend on the Holy Spirit to supply the power for our members to minister and witness? Could my church exist only on what God called our members to do? The answer is found throughout the New Testament: the Spirit's presence is made known in some way in each person for the good of all. Spiritual gifts are God's primary means of building a church.

# Corinth: The City

Seven Doric columns remain as mute monuments to the magnificence of ancient Corinth. The stillness contrasts with the stir of a once bustling cosmopolitan center where an international crowd, anticipating the vices of the city, jostled; where shoppers bargained in the *agora* (like a mall) over carpets, Lycaonian wool, or fine Corinthian ceramics; where fans filed into the stadium for the biennial Isthmian games; where worshipers repeated magical incantations to mythological gods; where the junction of major trade routes guaranteed commercial prosperity; where the migrant population of merchants, mariners, and travelers who heard the gospel could spread the Word over the world.

Silence reigns where the sounds of a complex society once filled the plain. The hammering of stone masons meant more embellishments to the columned courts, more marble-facade temples and marble gutters for expensive homes, another wine and cheese shop, or a monumental gateway. The chipping of stone by sculptors indicated another athlete, statesman, or god would adorn the Isthmian Avenue, a government building, or a temple.

Silence reigns where voices once filled the plain: debating philosophers and arguing students; butchers and temple priests compromising over the price of a goat offered at Apollo's temple; brawls; lewd songs of drunken revelry; the hysterical speaking of intoxicated women honoring Dionysus.

Corinthian citizens can best tell the story of their city. Let's meet a few.

*I am Plebus*, a dock worker at the port of Cenchreae. My crew sets small ships on rollers, drags them across the four-mile isthmus, and relaunches them on the other side. For large ships, the cargo is unloaded, carried by porters across land, and reloaded on another ship. Corinth, located on a strategic land strip, connects Peloponnesus with the Greek mainland.

Because of dangerous waters at the point of the peninsula mariners say, "Let him who sails around Malea (southern cape) forget home." Therefore, all sea traffic passes through the two harbors, making Corinth a trade and commercial center. The foreigners who disembark indulge in the varied pleasures and cults, particularly in the worship of Aphrodite, the goddess of love and beauty.

Sacred prostitutes ply their trade around the docks and are responsible for a familiar proverb, "It is not every man who can afford a journey to Corinth." Corinth has a hospitable reputation because of the city's accommodations and good water supply. Along with the other dock workers, the hotel keepers, cooks, and grooms, I take care of the needs of the travelers. We guide them down the Lechaion Road to the bronze images of the god Hermes, protector of travelers.

The dock workers, merchants, and sailors worship Poseidon, god of the sea. Believing that our fates rest in him, we pray, "Be kindly in heart and help those who voyage in ships," then we make sacrifices before his bronze image. Welcome to Corinth.

*I am Lais*, a courtesan from the cult of Aphrodite. She is a version of Asherah, the female consort of Baal in the ancient fertility religion of the Canaanites. In Corinth, religion is used to promote sex and fertility. Therefore, thousands of temple slaves have been dedicated to Aphrodite.

Being the companion of generals and statesmen, I lead an extravagant life-style. They lavish me with expensive homes and servants. Because of their generosity, my dressing table is crammed with mirrors, greasepaint, false hair, ribbons, neck chains, eye paint, and jewelry of precious stones. I am desired for my conversational skills and wit as well as my beauty. Because my clientele enjoy cultured women, courtesans have reserved seats in the theater. Our section is designated by a sign, "Belonging to the girls." Today I am sitting for a famous artist. He is painting my portrait to be hung in a public building. Socially, I am superior to the brothel slave girls and the common street walkers. Of course, I know that beauty fades and many former courtesans have starved to death. When I retire, I plan to sell or rent girls and boys for sexual purposes. At this moment, however, I am living for today. I am immaculate; my hair is tightly curled; my nails are polished; my purple dress is elegant. As I walk in the dust, my studded sandals spell "Follow Me!" Welcome to Corinth.

*I am Seneca*, a Roman. My great-grandfather was given a land grant when Julius Caesar rebuilt Corinth in 46 B.C. Today I own the family olive groves and vineyards tended by 120 slaves. Since present-day Corinth is only 100 years old, an aristocracy has not developed. I am of the "new rich" with enough money to bet on the Isthmian games, buy wine, and provide a regular sacrifice to Demeter, goddess of crops. Welcome to Corinth.

*My name is Pasion.* Captured in battle, I was brought to Corinth as a slave. By trade I am a skilled metalworker. I specialize in decorative handles for vases. My master gave me a business in the agora, and I guarantee him a percentage of the profits. Many slaves are accountants, estate managers, or librarians. Others are domestic servants. Everyday I walk to work on the marble Lechaion Road that is limited to pedestrian traffic. Often I stop to admire the ornamental gateway adorned with two gilded chariots carrying Helious, the sun god, and his son.

I belong to the Egyptian cult of Isis. This mystery religion is composed of both freemen and slaves who are disenchanted with the Greek gods. The Greeks do not offer us any reassurance in the hereafter. Isis promises immortal bliss once we have followed a ceremony that simulates death. Welcome to Corinth.

*I am Cleo* of the secluded sex, as women are called. As a

wife and mother I stay indoors, supervising the household, managing the slaves, and budgeting the money. I can leave the house to attend funerals and religious rites. On these occasions, my friends and I socialize. My father arranged my marriage. In the event of a separation, I have no legal standing. Also, adultery is tolerated in men but an automatic ground for divorce in women. My husband keeps slaves as concubines and a courtesan for companionship. I am only his housekeeper and child bearer.

I worship Cybele, a goddess from Asia Minor. In our worship we stand under a platform on which a bull is killed. His blood spills over us to atone for our sins. Welcome to Corinth.

*I am Epeirot*, a priest at the Asclepion, a center of healing. Asclepius was a mortal healer revived as a god. Our patients live in the temple, which is a sanatorium. They recline on stone benches for their ritual meals and enjoy the view and breezes from the gulf. Diet, exercise, baths, rest, prayer, meditation, and music prepare them for hypnotic dreams in which the god prescribes cures. As the priest, I use psychological means, including psychodrama, to heal. Inside the temple stands a white marble image of Asclepius, resting against a snake entwined staff. Thankful patients bring to the temple a terra cotta replica of the healed part of their body, which they place on an altar as an offering. Welcome to Corinth.

*I am Antigonus*, champion discus thrower. I have successfully competed against athletes from all over Greece to win the garland of pine needles. I was welcomed into the city through a special hole knocked in the wall. Then, accompanied by songs of praise, I was paraded through the streets. A statue, along with those of other victorious athletes, was erected in my honor along the stadium avenue. The Isthmian games, dedicated to Poseidon, begins with a sacrifice to him. His temple, built in a pine grove, contains his bronze image, standing with portrait statues of other athletes. In the past, the athletic discipline developed useful citizens. Now dishonesty in the training program produces idleness and immorality. Rather than a serious religious and athletic event, the games have degenerated to a carnival atmosphere. Welcome to Corinth.

*I am Erastus,* the city's chamberlain (treasurer). Since Corinth is the capital of the Roman province of Achaia, the proconsul, Gallio, and other government administrators reside in Corinth. A government appointment is a prized job. Politicians willing to leave Rome to work in the provinces become very wealthy. They are, however, expected to improve the city in a tangible way. In return for my appointment as chamberlain, I donated money to pave a road. Welcome to Corinth.

*I am Priscilla.* After my husband Aquila and I were expelled from Rome because of an anti-Semitic decree, we moved to Corinth. Many Jews, attracted by the commerce, live here. Being tentmakers, we began a business in the agora. Being Jews, we attended the local synagogue.

When Paul came to town, he found work and lodging with us. Through his witness, we found the Messiah as Saviour. Preaching to the polytheistic, philosophical, immoral Corinthians, Paul felt anxiety. However, during his eighteen month visit, he resolved "to know nothing . . . except Jesus Christ and Him crucified" (1 Cor. 2:2 NASB).

First he testified to the Jews. When they resisted and blasphemed, he left the synagogue declaring, "Now I will preach to the Gentiles." We Christians moved our place of worship to the home of Titius Justus, a Gentile. A vision reaffirmed Paul's commission: "Do not be afraid, keep on speaking, do not be silent. For I am with you"—even in Corinth. Paul obeyed. And the dock worker, the prostitute, the slave, and all the others who welcomed you to Corinth accepted Christ as Saviour. The Holy Spirit came to live in each life. The Corinthians became saints, separated from the ordinary, devoted to being God's possession. Welcome to our church in Corinth.

Read 1 Corinthians 5-6 and 8-11 to discover how the Corinthian culture and environment influenced the

Christians' behavior and affected the church. Fresh from a pagan society, the believers became babes in Christ. Still clinging to Corinthian ethics, to the philosophical partisan spirit of Greek democracy, and to dependence on human wisdom, the new Christians formed factions in the church. Lawsuits before heathen judges manifested their greed. Their gluttony and drunkenness debauched the Lord's table. Their idolatry and love of luxury enticed them to continue eating cult meals with pagan friends. The amoral feelings toward sex produced a lax attitude toward sexual misconduct of church members. Their new freedom in Christ gave them license to abuse their Christian liberty.

Paul did not seek to offer a solution to these problems through arbitrary rules. He stated principles which, based on love, have abiding value. Love demonstrated in unselfish consideration for others is the mark of the new life.

Still clinging to the ecstasies of pagan rites and to the belief that some devotees (followers of gods) were especially possessed by a deity, the new Christians desired an extraordinary experience with the Holy Spirit. Perhaps to demonstrate their new spirituality, they turned their Christian worship service into a display of their individual gifts. They vied for prominence, saying:

"Listen to my eloquence!"

"Listen to my ecstatic utterance!"

"Listen to my knowledge of spiritual things!"

They were ambitious for the more spectacular gifts. Their emphasis on the exciting elements caused them to miss God's Spirit in the experience of service in the fellowship.

Paul did not criticize their zeal and vitality. He recognized that the Holy Spirit had equipped these people with "every spiritual gift . . . for doing His will" (see 1 Cor. 1:7). He reminded them that their gifts were not personal endowments; they were intended to build up the church, to make it a strong witness in the city, to benefit every believer. He reminded them that one day the eloquence, utterances, and knowledge would end. Only love would remain.

To permeate their society with Christian principles posed difficult problems for the new Corinthian believers. Before we judge harshly our Corinthian brothers and sisters in Christ, pause and reflect: How does society influence our worship? How does our worship affect society?

# Corinth: The Christian Church

"God loves the church," proclaimed the pastor. Hearing that remark as a child, I imagined God enveloping all church buildings and congregations in one huge embrace. As an adult reading about the church at Corinth, I began wondering how God could love *that* church. Then, as my study of 1 Corinthians 12 progressed, I had a refreshing impression: "I love My church." *I* and *My* make the difference. God's love is personal. His embrace is just for you and me. In A.D. 54, God loved His church at Corinth so much that He endowed the members with every gift necessary for service.

## Welcome to the Church at Corinth

The citizens of Corinth were decadent, divisive, emotional, and enthusiastic. Ecstatic trances, uncontrolled speech, and frenzied physical abandonment characterized their pagan worship. Some of these Corinthians accepted Jesus as Saviour. When the Holy Spirit entered their lives, He gave them spiritual gifts which uniquely equipped them to serve God.

The spirit world was very real to the new Christians. Supernatural powers fascinated them. Even though they misunderstood the motives of the Holy Spirit and the purposes of the gifts, they allowed the Holy Spirit to work freely through them. These gifted folks generated a paradox of excitement and exhibitionism, vitality and vain glory, energy and envy. Recognizing that gifts were becoming a menace to their unity, they asked Paul for advice.

Having lived in Corinth for almost two years, Paul was gentle as he wrote, "I want you to know the truth about [gifts], my brothers" (1 Cor. 12:1*b* TEV).

In 1 Corinthians 12:4-7, Paul explained about the diversity of gifts, their common source, and their one purpose. The Holy Spirit gave each believer a gift to perform a necessary ministry. A particular gift makes the Spirit's reality obvious in a believer's life. Because of the variety of gifts, working through unique personalities, no Christian is a carbon copy of another.

These gifts make possible many ministries to benefit others. Rather than conflict, the ministries harmonize in service for the same Lord. The reality that factions existed in Corinth indicated the church's carnality and the members' abuse of their gifts.

When gifts operate within a congregation, we witness God's divine power at work. Because the endowments are called gifts of the Spirit, some believers tend to overlook the role of the Father and the Son in their functions and results. The Holy Spirit always magnifies Jesus Christ; Jesus always glorifies God. Each person of the Trinity is vitally related to the gifts.

We are individually endowed, but our gifts benefit the congregation. Gifts are not intended for personal fame or profit. They are not earned, not evidence of maturity or commitment, not a badge to display. Gifts are intended to edify the body of Christ, the church.

In 1 Corinthians 12:8-10, 28-30, Paul identified the gifts and functions existing in the Corinthian church. The list is not limiting; at other times Paul identified other gifts. The following gifts were important for him to mention to the church at this particular time.

When the church needed intelligent guidance, one member received a truth from God and conveyed His thoughts to the congregation. This gift of wisdom did not come after study or through human experience, but by revelation.

With the gift of knowledge, another received revelation of facts relating to a situation. This gift enabled a believer to discover and clarify ideas that were necessary for the growth of the church.

Because all Corinthian Christians experienced saving faith, all believers possessed the fruit of the Spirit, faithfulness, meaning dependablity. Yet one in the congregation had an indomitable trust in God. This individual with the gift of faith visualized a specific task that God wanted to accomplish. To make the vision a reality, he made decisions not based on logic or human understanding.

In the name of the Lord one commanded diseased bodies to be healed and God instantaneously healed through a human channel. Recuperation was unnecessary; the cure was immediately visible.

Still another exorcised demons and exercised power over nature. God used a human channel to show His supernatural power. Again, the results of the miracles were immediately visible.

One with the prophetic gift revealed the truth of the gospel. Understanding the will and intention of God, he warned, rebuked, advised, and guided. With authority, he spoke forth, "Thus saith the Lord." Eventually these messages became part of the content of our Bible.

To distinguish between the sincere and the sham was necessary in a society where abnormal occurrences were common. Another person was given the gift of discernment, identifying immediately whether a speaker was inspired by the Holy Spirit or influenced by Satan. God did not leave the church defenseless when false teachers appeared on the scene.

Someone else delivered a revelation of divine mysteries unintelligible to that person and to other worshipers. Still another perceived the meaning of unintelligible words. Sometimes he or she interpreted an exhortation; other times, a message magnifying God.

The gifts operated within an elementary structure identified by Paul in the order of the first three functions or positions of leadership. First, the itinerant apostles laid the doctrinal and structural foundation of the church. Prerequisites for an apostle included being with Jesus from the beginning of His ministry, being personally appointed by Christ, and witnessing the resurrection. Given special authority to be Christ's representatives, the apostles founded the early church. When they died, the apostolate ended.

The prophets came next in Paul's list and included the members who would communicate God's instruction to His church. Then came the teachers. These more mature leaders instructed believers in their faith. The gifts of the apostles, prophets, and teachers were profitable in producing spiritual growth. Then, as now, proclaiming Jesus Christ as Saviour was the central and vital mission of the church.

Still others were helpers. Not motivated by public recognition, helpers served because of unselfish concern. They ministered to physical needs, releasing the prophets and teachers for ministry to the spiritual needs of people.

Someone else was the administrator. This person coordinated the gifts of others in the best way to build up the church. The word *administer* means "to steer a ship through treacherous shoals." In Romans 12:8, Paul mentions the gift of ruling or leading. Not all leaders enjoy administering the day-to-day responsibilities of an organization. Administration could be a subtle refinement of the gift of leadership.

## Welcome to Your Church
The following situations show the parallel between the gifts and functions in the Corinthian church and in your church. Consider church members who exhibit these gifts. Affirm them by placing their names in the appropriate blank. Answering the questions which follow the situations will help you identify your own gift if it is included in the Corinthian list.

• *Wisdom:* When members reach an impasse in a business meeting, the one with the gift of wisdom chooses the proper action to settle the matter. Other members recognize that the truth was spoken. As a result, everyone ultimately agrees on a solution. The one with the gift of wisdom can remain distant from the emotions of the moment and listen to all opinions. Members appreciate the gifted one's sensitivity that helps them feel personal satisfaction and group togetherness. Members with this gift are problem solvers who feel confident their decisions harmonize with God's will. Those gifted with wisdom are trusted to hold confidences: they know when to speak and when to keep silent.

I affirm _____'s gift of wisdom.
Do you see clear answers to complex problems?
Do you have the ability to make wise decisions?

• *Knowledge:* The one gifted with knowledge likes to search the Scripture, analyze ideas, and gather and summarize facts. These facts discovered by the person with the gift of knowledge are applied to practical situations by the one with the gift of wisdom. The two work together well.

I affirm _____'s gift of knowledge.
Do you like to research or interpret biblical insights?

• *Faith:* People with the gift of faith express confidence that God will overcome any obstacle to the church's progress. They unconditionally ask of God, thank Him in advance, and look for an answer. Undaunted by impossible situations, they expect God to intervene. Members with this gift are impatient with critics and have unswerving confidence that they are doing God's will. Feeling a kinship to Noah, the one gifted with faith would build a boat in the Mohave Desert.

I affirm _____'s gift of faith.
Do you easily trust God in difficult circumstances?
Do you often wonder why people do not seem to know

God's will for their lives?

•*Prophesy:* Members who have the gift of prophesy proclaim with authority the intention of God. They apply the Word of God to social and moral issues. The information they share through speaking or writing strengthens, comforts, and encourages (see 1 Cor. 14:3). Laypersons as well as those in leadership positions can exercise this gift.

I affirm _____'s gift of prophesy.
Do you speak out to warn that Christian principles should apply to family life? athletics? politics? entertainment?
Do you often speak appropriate words to people at the exact time they need to hear those words?

•*Discernment:* Gifted discerners detect subtle errors mixed with truth in lectures, books, and mass media; they then warn the congregation of those errors. Members with this gift detect impostors who claim to speak the truth. They pierce through pretense to the true views and feelings of the false teacher.

I affirm _____'s gift of discernment.
Do you have the ability to detect false teachings or to "spot a phony"?

•*Helps:* Gifted helpers shun the limelight, but delight in driving the handicapped or the elderly to appointments. The helper assists, lends a hand, sees and meets needs. Helpers enjoy preparing for events by cleaning, cooking, or decorating. They like to arrange flowers or organize sheet music for the choir.

I affirm _____'s gift of helps.
Do you volunteer for the unnoticed activities that help your church?

Do you feel good when you help with routine church jobs?

•*Administrator* (governing): The gifted administrator is a take-charge, goal-oriented person who expresses the gift with tact and humility. The result is harmony in the body. This person has spiritual authority but is never domineering nor dictatorial. Being able to identify the gifts of others, she or he delegates, organizes, and uses resources of the local body. Usually one group in a church is traditional, another inventive. The administrator advises others when to be preserving and when to be innovative.

I affirm _____'s gift of administration.

Do you enjoy organizing and leading projects and activities?

Do you like to motivate others to be their best?

•*Apostle:* In a restricted sense, this gift ended when the last apostle died. In a broader sense, missionaries who cross cultures and plant churches have the same strong sense of mission.

I affirm _____'s openness to follow God's will wherever He leads.

Do you feel at ease with people of different cultures, races, or languages? Are you willing to go anywhere God wants to send you?

•*Prophets*: Refer to the discussion of prophecy.

•*Teachers*: The gifted teacher has the ability to share Bible truths in a way that causes members to apply the teachings to daily life. Gifted teachers create a learning atmosphere and speak the Word of God clearly and accurately.

I affirm _____'s gift of teaching.

Do you spend extra time studying the Bible so that you can explain it simply to others?

•*Healing and Miracles*: As the tumor pressed against her spine, many people prayed for God to heal her. The doctors read the second scan of her spine, looked perplexed, re-examined earlier x-rays, and declared, "The tumor has disappeared."

No member of the congregation came forward to verbally command the tumor to dissolve. No member, by spoken word, intervened to overrule the laws of nature and add years to the woman's life.

God did! Divine healers are not evident to any measurable degree within today's churches. But divine healing is a reality. God still performs miracles even though His channel is not usually a gifted person in a congregation.

The Mexican Mazatec's definition of miracles is "long necked things." They cause us to stretch our necks to see something amazing. Astonishing events and experiences still occur. In a broad sense, remarkable answers to prayer, superhuman strength, unexplainable events, or timely protection are miracles.

My friend's experience with a tumor does not prove or disprove the gifts of healing and miracle working. However, these are very rare gifts, perhaps even in a state of quiescence at this time. Healings and miracles clustered around critical periods in biblical history: the Exodus; the prophets; Christ; the early church. Through these unusual manifestations, God confirmed the gospel and authenticated His spokesmen. Today, and in the future, if critical periods were to occur in the advancement of the gospel, God could activate these gifts. By decreeing that healing and miracle working were only first century phenomena, we deny the sovereignty of God.

## Misusing Gifts

When you look at your church's body, do you see an orderly blend of different gifts? Or do you see a huge hand out of proportion to the rest of the body? Everyone wants to help. No one wants to teach. Do you see a big mouth? Everyone wants to prophesy. No one wants to discern. Do you see busy feet? Everyone wants to run around administering. No one wants to listen to others' opinions.

The body of Christ at Corinth resembled a tongue. As you read 1 Corinthians 14, imagine you are seated in a public worship service at Corinth. One gift, coveted above the others, deformed the body. The incoherent murmurs and strange words did not cause the church's disgraceful conduct and immature attitudes (see 1 Cor. 1:7,11,15). However, within the unstable church, speaking in tongues was the gift most highly prized. In all of Paul's letters, only once did he speak of this gift, and that was because of its abuse.

All the gifts were valuable; but some, like prophecy, ranked higher in edification. *Edification*, an old-fashioned word we would do well to reclaim for our vocabulary, suggests a constructiveness that strengthens life. Both a motive and a measure for service, edification includes love, which helps to build up individuals as well as the fellowship. The test for using any gift should be, "Does it edify the body?"

In public worship, intelligible communication benefits everyone more than ecstatic utterances. Through a series of contrasts, Paul shows the supremacy of prophecy that leads men to say, "Jesus is Lord." Every statement in 1 Corinthians 14 about speaking in tongues is followed by a contrasting appeal to cultivate the gift of prophecy.

•*Contrast 1* (vv. 2-3): "The one who speaks in strange tongues does not speak to others but to God" (TEV). Unintelligible prayers were not messages to the congregation, nor were they designed for communication with God. They were given so that believers could reveal God to people. Listeners to those who spoke in tongues were able to hear sounds, but they were unable to distinguish the messages God wanted to give.

"But the one who proclaims God's message speaks to

people and gives them help, encouragement, and comfort" (v. 3). Before the Gospels were available, prophecies conveyed God's truth to the church. One gift, prophecy, equipped believers to live the Christian life (edification), cheered the depressed, strengthened a person's determination to reach desired goals (encouragement), and soothed the sorrowing (comfort).

•*Contrast 2* (v. 4): "The one who speaks in strange tongues helps only himself" (v. 4*a* TEV). Striving for spiritual maturity is a constant goal for every Christian. However, gifts were not given for an inward spiritual experience or to benefit self. A by-product of using any gift to help others will be the blessing that comes to the helper. But if the goal is self-edification, the motive is questionable.

"But the one who proclaims God's message helps the whole church" (v. 4*b*). A prophet communicates understandable truth to all the congregation, which is the purpose of spiritual gifts.

•*Contrast 3* (v. 5): "I would like for all of you to speak in strange tongues" (v. 5*a* TEV). According to 1 Corinthians 12, for all to have the same gift is contrary to God's purpose for His body. By this statement, Paul made the point that he valued all the gifts.

Overstatement sometimes characterized Paul's writings. For example, in 1 Corinthians 7:7, he wished for all to remain single; but he knew that most people would marry.

"But I would rather that you had the gift of proclaiming God's message" (v. 5*b*). Spontaneously, an inspired prophet would explain a spiritual insight that the congregation could understand. A tongues speaker's message had value to edify only when it was interpreted to the congregation.

•*Contrast 4* (vv. 18-19): "I thank God that I speak in strange tongues much more than any of you" (v. 18 TEV). Since Paul was endowed with both gifts, he could, from personal experience, evaluate the benefits of the gifts to the church.

"But in church worship I would rather speak five

words that can be understood, in order to teach others, than speak thousands of words in strange tongues." A few words that will develop Christian maturity are superior to an endless number that only give spiritual and emotional pleasure to an individual. The value of public worship is destroyed if people are unable to understand the message about God. Public worship should encourage the participation of all present.

Helpful communication must transmit understanding, not merely produce sounds. To support the contrasts, Paul used examples from actual life (vv. 7-11). Musical instruments were played at funerals, religious ceremonies, and banquets. Notes played together in appropriate patterns created a mood of joy or grief. A listener could recognize and appreciate the melody. From these same instruments, irregular vibrations produced useless noise.

In the military, simply blowing a trumpet was insufficient. Distinctions and repetitions in the sound designated courses of action to be taken. Soldiers would not respond to an indefinite bugle blast. In public worship, speaking in tongues is like a garbled flute, an indistinct trumpet, or foreign words. Without an interpretation, tongues are vain and unprofitable.

•*Contrast 5* (vv. 21-25): "So then the gift of speaking in strange tongues is proof for unbelievers, not for believers" (v. 22*a* TEV). What tongues may "prove" to unbelievers is that "you are all insane." Skeptical outsiders, without knowledge of the Holy Spirit, would believe that Christians were filled with a god who drove them insane, as they thought gods did in their pagan orgies.

In contrast, prophecy produced faith in unbelievers, making them believers. When the gospel is preached, the Holy Spirit convicts, judges, and reveals the heart's true condition. The results are repentance and worship (vv. 24-25).

No one yawned in the Corinthian church! Christians who attended church were determined to speak. Verse 26 lists some of the elements of their worship. Variety of gifts did not always mean edification. Without an order of service, each member contributed when thy felt the urge. The consequence of their zeal was rivalry and abuse of gifts. By placing limitations on the tongues speakers and prophets, Paul attempted to quell the confusion without quenching their enthusiasm.

These restrictions (vv. 27-28) guaranteed the profitable use of tongues: (1) No more than three persons must speak, and then one at a time. (2) Interpretation must follow each message. (3) If no interpreter was present, the tongues speaker must be silent.

These regulations (vv. 29-31) governed the gift of prophecy: (1) Again, no more than three persons were to speak, one at a time. (2) Those with the gift of discernment must judge the accuracy of the message. (3) One prophet should stop speaking when another was given fresh insight.

Notice that tongues speakers and prophets could control their gifts (v. 32). Pagan priests were compelled to speak as long as the demon spirit possessed them. In Christian worship, lack of restraint could not be blamed on the gift, but on the self-assertive person who wanted recognition. Self-control is evident as a fruit in the Spirit-controlled life (see Gal. 5:22-23).

A gathering of Christians does not automatically mean worship. If the assembly is characterized by confusion caused by members who are puffed up and insist on having their way, it is not of God. "God does not want us to be in disorder but in harmony and peace" (v. 33 TEV).

Sweetness and symmetry permeate the gathering of Christians who pursue love and who place all the gifts in subjection to love for one another (v. 40). In this atmosphere, worship causes believers to fall on their knees in praise, and unbelievers in repentance. The articulate message causes a community to respond, "God is really there among you" ( v. 25 NIV).

We must guard against making one gift supreme and using it to measure the spiritual depth of every member.

Overemphasis on any of the gifts (not necessarily related to tongues) may cause division and dogmatism in the church. Make your prayer, "My dear brothers, let love be our greatest aim."

# Corinth: The Christian Church — A Gifted Body

Next door to the Jewish synagogue, in the home of Titius Justus, the Corinthian believers gathered to worship. Occasionally, as they strolled past the synagogue, they may have heard the Jews taunt, "Your Jesus is no Christ. God's curse be on Him."

The new Christians recently confessed, "Jesus is Lord" and forsook their demon inspired worship to gods that could not see or hear (see 1 Cor. 12:2). The pagan priests encouraged them to believe that the most spirit-filled devotees would reach the most uncontrollable delirium of excitement. These new Christians were not immediately weaned from equating emotional ecstasies with the presence of the Spirit.

Possibly in the excitement of using their gifts in the intense, electric worship of God, someone shrieked, "A curse on Jesus." I imagine such a curse would have stung Paul when he learned of it. As the persecutor, Saul had attempted to force believers to blaspheme God. The inexperienced Christians assumed that the curse indicated divine inspiration. "Not so," declared Paul.

The Holy Spirit never inspires an ecstatic cry of unbelief. Submission to the Lordship of Christ, not a heightened emotional outburst, is evidence of the Holy Spirit's presence. The Holy Spirit always inspires the intelligible confession that "Jesus is Lord." His primary task in A.D. 54 and today is to convince people to confess Jesus as Lord. No doubt the name "Lord" stirred frightening thoughts in the believers' minds. Caesar demanded their allegiance as "Lord Caesar." To declare that "Jesus is Lord" in their pagan society required the Holy Spirit inspired fruit of faithfulness.

41

Influenced by the competitiveness of their corrupt culture and their immoral cults, the new believers were confused about how to use their many gifts. Their vitality endangered their worship. Still having a fondness for the spectacular, they competed for prominence. Comparison of gifts led to rivalry.

When Paul's letter arrived they read, "The Spirit's presence is shown in some way in each person for the good of all" (1 Cor. 12:7 TEV). This concept startled folks who sought individual preeminence. The members gossiped in the corridors: Is Paul serious? Are we gifted to bless others? Slowly they learned that their gifts demonstrated God's grace, which eliminated any basis for pride.

Paul borrowed an illustration from their Latin tradition to picture the unity of the varied gifts. Roman historians compared the political state to a human body. The philosopher Plato compared the body to a city. For the Corinthians, unfamiliar with the Hebrew covenant concept, the body was an appropriate symbol of unity.

## God's Creation: The Human Body

Beth, suffering from an inner ear infection, staggered into the doctor's office. After stumbling into her chair, she overheard another patient remark, "She should be at Alcoholics Anonymous." We take for granted the unity of our physical body until one part does not function properly. Read 1 Corinthians 12:12-26 from a physiological point of view. Keep in mind that the body, an organic whole, is composed of many parts performing different functions.

Many years before Paul wrote to the Corinthians, David marveled, "I will praise thee; for I am fearfully and wonderfully made" (Psalm 139:14*a* KJV). Housed within a skeletal frame, seven different intricate systems and a variety of glands and organs function. Each part has a particular job and the parts cooperate to keep the body alive.

In God's design:
• One body part does not constitute the whole body.
• The parts do not complain about their place in the body.

• The parts do not compare their functions. Internal organs, while vital to life, are not depreciated in their value by the handicap of an amputated arm.
• When the parts function properly, the whole body enjoys health. When any one part hurts, other parts register discomfort. Sometimes a healthy part must compensate for an injured part.
• God is responsible for balance among the parts.

## God's Creation: The Spiritual Body

God created His spiritual body, the church. Paul wrote, "God put every different part in the body just as He wanted it to be. In the church God has put all in place" (1 Cor. 12:18, 28a TEV). Just as God created balance in the parts of the human body, so He assigned members a place in a spiritual body. You are where you are by divine appointment. You are important because God uniquely gifted you for ministry. This fact gives dignity to each one, no matter how small or how great the gift. Outstanding ministries indicate our abilities, but small services show the depth of commitment.

Making a spiritual application of 1 Corinthians 12:12-18 helps us understand Paul's advice on the proper use of gifts. In God's design, the church is the body of Christ. Comparing the church to the human body is not a mere analogy. The church is the spiritual body of Christ. The persecutor, Saul, devastated the church. Yet on the Damascus Road the Lord's question was, "Why are you persecuting me?" (Acts 9:4b NASB).

The body of Christ is composed of people with many abilities, enabling them to minister in a variety of ways. The Holy Spirit blends our differences into a unique unity without stereotyping individuals. He preserves the individuality of personalities.

For example, in your church, several people may be gifted teachers. Because of their personalities, one may relate to children; another to adults. Several people may be gifted helpers. One enjoys hosting the fellowships and meals; another likes to prepare bulletin boards or collect egg cartons for Bible school. A healthy body accepts the differences in others.

In God's design, a new believer does not stand alone, but is immediately joined to the body of Christ through the baptism of the Holy Spirit. Members are composed of many different temperaments, tastes, and talents. They transcend all ethnic, religious, and social distinctions. A church fragmented by prejudice or infiltrated by the false standards of society is not true to God's plan for the body. In God's design, mutual dependence of members characterizes the church.

After introducing the subject, Paul changes the focus from the whole body to individual parts. Fretful foot complains, "All I do is support body weight. Graceful hand caresses a child, paints a portrait, or stirs a gourmet dessert. Compared to the complex skills of hand, I am inferior. I will secede from the body."

Intimidated ear begrudges the beauty and perception of the eye. "Naturally you receive compliments because you are set in a prominent place. On the side of the head, I'm either unnoticed or the target of unflattering jokes. I'm unimportant. I will secede from the body."

While these members succumb to self-pity, others overestimate their importance. Conspicuous eye is contemptuous of hand. Big brain gloats over little nerve. Arrogant head feels superior to lowly feet.

Silly body! If you were an ear, I could never see a sunset. If you were an eye, I could never hear a symphony. If you were a foot, I could never be still. And don't you know that if a brier penetrates the foot, a tiny nerve signals the brain, which alerts the entire body? Don't you know that when you win a race, the wreath is placed on your head, and not around your feet?

Paul reminded these confused believers that if any of them secede, or usurp the honor due another, they would atrophy, decay, and die. Those believers endowed with grand gifts were applauded and admired. They developed a haughty superiority, saying, "We can run this church." Christians endowed with modest gifts were ignored. Feeling that their gifts were worthless, they said to the honored crowd, "Go ahead and run the church."

Foolish folks! If everyone prophesies, who will organize? If everyone discerns, who will help? If everyone speaks with wisdom, who will teach? Variety in the church is not accidental. If all members exercised the same gift, the church would be deformed. Think of the mixed-up menus and kitchen confusion if every woman who has the gift of helping desired to be the hostess.

In God's design, each member is necessary. Paul addressed the problem of wrangling about the importance of certain gifts. The Christians who did not possess the coveted gifts underestimated the importance of their own gifts. They became discontented with themselves and envious of the members with more conspicuous gifts. Pouting, they were tempted to deprive the body of their ministry. Paul explained that complaining will not remove the individual from the body. The body of Christ cannot operate at peak efficiency if one believer becomes inactive or refuses to use his or her gift. No matter how small the gift seems, each member is necessary to the life of the church. Ministering with your gift makes you valuable.

Notice the number of times *I* is used in these verses. "I" was one of the problems. If we focus our gifts on ourselves, they will not fulfill their proper purpose of building up the church. Believers who bicker and criticize disillusion others in the body.

To think that one person could be the whole church is as absurd as thinking one leg can be the whole human body. No matter how gifted, one believer cannot perform all the ministries or functions of the body. The questions in verse seventeen point out the necessity for diversity. Each member has something to offer; none has everything. God's design keeps the body from being a monstrosity.

In God's design members do not depreciate one another. Those who are unobserved in the background may appear weak; however, significance is not based on appearance or activity. The fact that our lungs and liver are unseen does not diminish their significance. The kidneys and brain are not as comely as finely chiseled facial features or lithe limbs, but who can survive without them? The glamorous gifts are dependent on gifts that seem weak. Teachers depend on those with the helping gifts to arrange the room or plan the socials. Evangelists depend on those with the gift of faith to claim God's promises and intercede until answers come.

In God's design, all members are honored. Have you ever complained about chubby feet or narrow heels? Thick or thin hips? A prominent nose or projecting ears? On our human bodies, we find ways to conceal less attractive features with fashionable shoes, vertical or horizontal stripes, cosmetics, or hair styles. In doing so we actually pay greater attention to "those parts we think aren't worth very much" (1 Cor. 12:23a TEV). To those in the body of the church who lack prominent or esteemed gifts, God gives extra honor. God arranges the gifts so that all members receive recognition.

God's design prevents scorn, schisms, clashes, jealousy, and superiority/inferiority feelings. Perhaps the Corinthian citizens had heard this fable by Livy, the Roman historian: "Once upon a time, members of the body had a grievance against the belly because it did nothing but enjoy what they bestowed upon it. They struck work but soon found that they were really starving themselves. This made it clear to them that even the belly nourished the other members while it was being nourished by them." Harmony, not rivalry, exists in the body when all members faithfully minister to one another through their unique gifts.

In God's design, empathy promotes togetherness in the body. Pain in one part destroys the peace of the whole body. When a physical ailment threatens the health of a friend, we rush to console or comfort. Likewise, when frustrations nag at one member like a grain of sand in a shoe; when unalterable circumstances crush the initiative of another; when fatigue from 24-hour watchcare saps the strength of one; when tragedy tears a family apart; when a series of failures traps still another in a dead-end maze; when hurts and disappointments cause disillusionment, members of the spiritual body do not condemn and judge. They cry.

One member receives a job promotion; another makes a profitable career move; still another gains recognition for community service; another's child is voted "Miss or Mr. Everything." Members in the spiritual body do not criticize and demean; they rejoice. As much as we are able, we identify with each others' joys and sorrows.

In God's design, Christians working together become Christ's body. We each have a distinct place. If each member had every gift, we would be complete within ourselves, and independent of other members. The body would be useless. In God's design, diversity is necessary for the body to function. Unity without diverse gifts produces a monotonous uniformity, stifles fresh ideas, and crushes creativity. On the other hand, we learned from the Corinthian church that diversity without unity produces disorder and chaos. What balances unity and diversity? Love!

Jesus glorified God through His perfect human body. Ministering through a diversity of gifts, Jesus showed the love, the goodness, and the might of God. Many years ago in Corinth and today in your town or city, Jesus has a body that consists of living members. In every church, the variety of gifted believers has the power to change an almost lifeless or dead organization into a loving, good, mighty organism.

Almost like a postscript Paul adds, "Earnestly desire the greater gifts" (1 Cor. 12:31 NASB). Within the sovereignty of the Holy Spirit there is a place for earnest ambition that glorifies God. All parts of the human body are genuine. But in a particular instance, as when smelling a rose, the nose is more important than the ear. On the other hand, the lungs must always breathe. Functionally, the parts of the human body do not have equal voice.

Similarly, all spiritual gifts are real and necessary. However, they do not contribute equally all the time to the message and mission of the church. The greatest gift could be the one most needed at a particular time. By appreciating the gifts of others and faithfully using our own, we prepare ourselves to receive other gifts. However, in his writings, Paul consistently emphasized the gifts of preaching and teaching. Regardless of the many ministries our gifts enable us to perform, our greatest privilege is to share verbally our faith in Jesus Christ and to lead persons to confess, "Jesus, Lord!"

## Meditation: Hands and Feet!

Jesus' hands hammered, healed the sick, held a cup offered by an adulterous woman, turned over the money changers' tables, broke bread to feed multitudes, wiped away tears. One day they carried a cross.

His feet walked on dusty roads and on the water, stood on hillside slopes and before magistrates, carried Him to Lazarus's tomb and into the garden to pray. One day they trudged up Calvary's hill.

Because of love for you and me, Jesus allowed the spikes to penetrate His hands and feet.

Today you and I are His hands and feet. But taking His message and touching His people is in vain unless we take and touch because of love.

# Rome: The City

As a fascinated tourist, I stood on the Sacred Way, the main street of ancient Rome. The ruins resembled a desecrated cemetery: toppled columns, crumbling arches, decapitated statues. Facades of temples stood like regal sentries protecting decay. The stone stumps that witnessed the birth of a civilization now mark its grave—tombstones memorializing past grandeur.

Once these bits and pieces of granite and marble had flanked the Sacred Way as a grandiose complex of administrative, political, and judicial buildings, illustrious temples, and an imposing commercial center. Within the structures, the designs and schemes of men spawned an empire. The Roman Forum pulsated as the nerve center of the world.

When Paul stood on the flint stone Sacred Way, life flourished in and around the Forum. Two hundred sixty-five narrow streets wound through Rome. By day, pedestrians crowded the cobblestone passageways, representing a microcosm of the Roman world. At dusk, they disappeared inside to escape reckless drivers and garbage thrown from the windows. By nightfall the streets, closed to vehicles during business hours, were crammed with wagons delivering supplies to shops. The clatter of wheels and curses of the drivers created a constant racket, prompting the comment that Romans died from lack of sleep.

By meeting a few of the one to four million people who lived in the city, we can learn about the society in which the Roman Christians lived. We can learn of the everyday lives of the people to whom Paul wrote about spiritual gifts. Welcome to Rome.

49

*I am Domus,* one among the thousands of folks who value idleness. The elite citizens call my kind "the rabble." My favorite loitering place is the Forum. Sitting on the steps of the Temple of Vesta in the Sacred Way, my friends and I enjoy people-watching. We gossip about the palace scandals and complain about the housing shortage, high rent, and air pollution.

I pass the time playing backgammon on the marble platforms or scratching graffiti on the statues. I used to work for the government postal system. I traveled with a relay team, carrying messages to Puteoli. Because I wanted to travel more, I became a private messenger for a business. Their carriers changed horses at posting houses along the routes. When my boss replaced his hired workers with slaves, I became one of the idle.

Probably because of my experience in the postal service, the highlight of every day is the posting of the censored news sheet. From it everyone reads the proclamations, lists of births, obituaries, and announcements of public events.

From our vantage point, we idlers can view the state and municipal officials and the aristocrats in their coming and going from the senate house. Graft is so common among these people that it is taken for granted. Welcome to Rome.

*I am Pedarious,* a businessman with offices in the commercial center, Basilica Aemilia. Specifically I am a moneychanger, an important occupation in the Forum. Lending money is a profitable business. Heavy taxation and extravagant spending cause huge debts. The interest rate on borrowed money is 8 ⅓ percent. Some money changers charge one percent per month. "Money makes the man" is the materialistic concept of the day. Most employed people work until noon, then spend the afternoon shopping, debating at the Rostra, or bathing in the public baths. Even though our workday is short, we celebrate 159 holidays each year.

Unemployment is high. The availability of slaves contributes to this problem. Public slaves form 80 percent of the government's work force. Slave labor has ousted many peasants from farm jobs. Flocking to the city to find work, these peasants have joined the vast number of vagrants who congregate in the Forum. Welcome to Rome.

*I am Apelles,* an aristocrat who owns a bakery. Since common labor is considered socially inferior, one of my slaves operates the business. A baker's sign showing a mule turning a mill to grind grain designates my business in the shopping center. Customers say my round loaves of bread are the best in the city. The bush sign next door indicates a wine shop; a hireling works for that shop's owner. Since the government encourages competition and individual enterprise, shop keepers and craftsmen advertise. As you entered Rome on the Appian Way or the Flaminian Way, you probably noticed our signs etched in the stone tablets along the road ways.

In our shops, we also sell products manufactured by people we conquer. For example, Pergamum provides us with linens, wool, and parchment. Phoenicia sends silk, and Alexandria supplies us with perfumes. Besides necessities like oil used in lamps and for cooking and washing, shopkeepers sell exotic items like Black Sea sturgeon and African ostrich feathers.

Smoking shops offering ready-cooked takeout food thrive during the lunch hour. Barbers, furniture dealers, booksellers, and cloth merchants prosper alongside pharmacists and poultry sellers. Each profession is organized into a trade guild to benefit the workers; each guild worships a patron deity. In elections for municipal officials, the guilds support certain candidates. Their block vote often determines the results. However, because of lack of interest in politics, most citizens do not vote. Welcome to Rome.

*I am Daphnis,* a homemaker. At age 17, I married a noble man chosen by my parents. Even though I have no legal rights, I am held in high respect. Unlike other women who live within our empire, Roman women are free to shop, visit, and attend public functions.

Physical appearance is very important to us. At least once a week, I use a meal mask to smooth facial wrinkles. My colorful *stolas* (long tunics) are secured with fancy clasps. Fine jewelry is a must for the well dressed woman; rings adorn each finger. Curling irons and hair dyes powdered with gold dust help me create elaborate hairstyles. Since I have dark hair, I made myself a wig for variety, using the blond hair of my Germanic slave.

My main responsibility is to manage the household, including the family's five hundred slaves. I keep the storeroom keys, an important job. Since home management is the only training females receive, my mother taught me to be an excellent housekeeper.

A flippant attitude toward marriage prevails in Rome. In some instances couples agree to live together without a ceremony. Divorce is as quick as saying, "Take your own property, give up the keys to the storeroom, and be gone." The birthrate has decreased so much that the government pays a stipend to families with three children, and imposes a tax on bachelors.

One of our educated slaves tutors our young children. In some social classes, fathers teach their sons the family trade. Since my husband is wealthy, our six-year-old son will attend school away from home, but not necessarily in an educational facility since school buildings have not been constructed. Teachers meet wherever they find space and shelter. His courses will include physical exercise, rhetoric, oratory, and literature. Perhaps, when he is older, he will be able to study philosophy in Athens.

To escape the noise of the city, we own a home in the suburbs. The decor expresses a simple elegance. Rooms with tile floors and ceilings are arranged around an atrium. Murals and frescoes of landscapes and mythological scenes decorate the walls. In addition to a water system for domestic use, a pool in the atrium catches rain water from a vent in the roof. Instead of a sitting room, our house has a reclining room where we converse and eat.

Central heating is an added comfort. Three meals a day and a mid-afternoon snack are prepared in charcoal ovens. Homemakers without kitchens take their uncooked meals to a public oven. A simple breakfast of cheese served with bread dipped in wine is followed by a light lunch of an egg dish and fruit. Our three to seven course evening meal, usually lasting several hours, might include fish, poultry, pork, eggs, vegetables, nuts, and fruit. From the Greeks we learned to substitute olive oil for butter, and honey for sugar. When we invite dinner guests, they bring their napkins to use for taking home leftovers, a practice considered to be good manners.

For amusement the family enjoys variety shows at the amphitheaters featuring acrobats, dancers, and magicians. At smaller theaters we adults watch Greek drama performances of low farce and pantomime. We participate in the activities at one of the 170 public baths. The complex includes a gymnasium where bathers choose hot, luke-warm, or cold baths, saunas, and massages. An art gallery, public library, and shopping area connect to the baths.

Fathers are authoritative figures. The state encourages the authority of the father over the children. Officials feel that disciplined families ensure a disciplined state. Also, fathers serve as priests in family worship. Tiny statues of Lares and Penates, spirits of the home and hearth, occupy little shrines. We pray to them before meals and before important ventures. I worship Vesta, Rome's goddess of the hearth. Welcome to Rome.

*I am Epe*, a slum dweller. In contrast to wealthy homes, the disease-infested wooden tenements where I live cover miles of slum areas in the city. These six-storied, poorly constructed houses often collapse or catch fire. I depend on charity, theft, and gambling for my livelihood. To keep us from revolting, the government doles out grain, and sometimes money. The give-away program actually encourages laziness and loss of initiative. Welcome to Rome.

*I am Ampliatus*, a slave. Fifteen years ago, when I was a

strong teenager, my parents sold me in an auction. I'll never forget that day as I stood lined up with other non-citizens: prisoners of war, an assortment of seafaring folks sold by pirates, little children, condemned criminals. Noblemen at the auction bought us for tens of thousands of dollars.

Slaves choke the streets and hang out around the houses of the wealthy, clamoring for a handout. For fear we will become aware of our strength, the government does not furnish uniforms or brand us. The exception is an "F" branded on the forehead of a fugitive.

I work at the amphitheater. Beneath the wooden floor, I maneuver machines that pull animal cages up to the level of the sand covered arena floor. Some of the slaves who are brought to Rome as prisoners from other parts of the empire are highly skilled professional people. Slave accountants work in the commercial center. Others are architects and master builders who travel the empire erecting aqueducts and building roads. Some slaves are expert sculptors, beautifying the city with columns and arches that are decorated with carvings and reliefs of Rome's conquests. Other slave artists have studios where they sculpt portrait busts of citizens.

Most slaves are treated as inanimate objects and I have heard of inhumane treatment, although some become like family to kind owners. In this time of Roman peace, the slave supply from conquered lands is low. To fill the gap, some slaves are bred like cattle. Welcome to Rome.

*I am Stachys*, a *pagani*, or farmer. Agriculture is regarded as the only suitable occupation for a gentleman. For many years I employed peasants to work the farm. In recent years, to save money, I replaced the peasants with slaves. I allow a few of the best-trained slaves to sell the produce they tend and give me a percentage. They can accumulate enough savings to buy their freedom within about six years.

Farming is becoming more and more difficult. Because Rome depends on imports for necessities, shipping is big business. In fact, small farmers could not match the lower prices of imported food. Some became tenant farmers; others remain unemployed.

Farm families celebrate two main festivals: seed time, and harvest time. On those days we ask the god of the field and sky to bless our crops. I'm proud to say that we farmers remained faithful to our gods and were the last to accept Christianity. Because we were steadfast in our opposition, non-Christians are called pagans. Welcome to Rome.

*I am Flavia*, a gladiator. So far I am a survivor in the organized carnage called a sports event. Athletic sports and drama, such as the Greeks enjoy, are too tame for the Romans. We delight in unequal matches: a gladiator versus a lion, a dwarf against a woman, archers versus panthers, rival gladiators against one another. Usually, gladiators fight until one dies. Twice in my career, spectators spared my life from an opponent's fatal spearing. A rule in our game allows spectators to save the life of their favorite gladiator by waving their handkerchiefs.

One of Emperor Nero's favorite match-ups is soldiers fighting 400 bears. Animals, captured in Africa, are shipped to Rome for the contests. Killing 5,000 animals in one day is not unusual. Nero always makes each amusement that he sponsors more frenzied than the last.

Intermissions are frequent while slaves add fresh sand to the blood-soaked arena. "The bloodier, the better" is the cry of the crowd who watch the brutality, while munching sausages and swigging drinks. Nero justifies the cruelty by saying he is hardening citizens to the sight of bloodshed so they can endure war.

Since I am a successful gladiator, I am housed in special barracks, carefully fed, and receive medical attention. I travel and fight in the provinces where Greek theaters have been converted into arenas for our show. I hope I live long enough to retire and maybe become a senator. Welcome to Rome.

*I am Rufus*, a famous charioteer. Being a popular hero, I

earn huge sums of money. Fans crowd the roads as they follow me or another favorite chariot team all over the empire. In Rome we race in the Circus Maximus, a three storied structure covered with marble. Crowds of 250,000 fans, obtaining cushions and programs at the gate, place bets on their favorite racer. Wildly rooting for their team, supporters occasionally are crushed in the crowd.

Charioteers race around a central barrier in the middle of the Circus Maximus. The gigantic barrier holds an Egyptian obelisk, fountains, statues of dignitaries, and a device to help spectators count the laps. We are heroes to children, who mimic adult games. They spear rabbits instead of bears and are pulled by goats or dogs. Teachers complain that the children prefer sports to studies.

Gambling is evident at all the amusements. A popular saying is "panem et Circenses" (bread and circus games), for free food and entertainment are the major interests of the people. The government sponsors the demoralizing events to appease the unemployed. Welcome to Rome.

*I am Seneca*, a Stoic philosopher and Nero's former tutor. The tenets of Stoicism have evolved through the years to the principles I espouse. From the Forum Rostra, I teach these beliefs: logos, the organizing force, formed the universe; the ability to reason is human's highest achievement; good persons reach out to God; individuals are capable of reaching moral perfection in their own strength; sin is a lack of knowledge; evil does not exist; all people have certain basic rights; class distinction and slavery are immoral; self-control, soberness, wisdom, and justice are primary virtues. One residue of original stoicism is imbedded in my mind. I believe that death cures all ills and to choose suicide is the highest privilege. I preach, "Do you see your neck, your throat, your heart? These are the places of salvation." Welcome to Rome.

*I am Claude*, a Legionnaire who has just reenlisted for another 20 years to serve in the infantry. The military constantly travels the Roman roads, which originate at the Forum. The golden milestone on the Sacred Way indicates the distance to every city in the Empire. When we are not fighting or patrolling, we build bridges, aqueducts, roads, and walls. Some soldiers serve as firemen in Rome. My career goal is to be handpicked to join the Praetorian Guard, serving the emperor. However, regardless of individual rank, the Roman army is prestigious. Our presence in every city and town and on every frontier ensures Roman peace. Welcome to Rome.

*I am Galen*, a priest in the Temple of Vesta, goddess of fire. Vesta protects the hearths in our homes and in our state. In the Forum, I manage the public hearth and supervise the work of six Vestal Virgins. They live in a large house adjacent to the temple. Because citizens highly esteem the vestals, their house is a depository for important documents. The Vestal Virgins guard the sacred fire, which burns continually. When people leave Rome, they take some of the coals with them to start a fire in their new home.

Times are changing. Old religions are dying daily; the thousands of ancient Roman gods have degenerated to a few. To the average citizen, the gods of the Greek and Roman pantheon are old fashioned. Because of Roman conquests, many "new" gods have temples in the city. The government tolerates foreign deities, so long as they are not a menace to the empire's unity.

The government insists that all citizens worship the three national deities who would prosper the state: Jupiter, controller of the weather; Ceres, controller of the harvest; and Mars, controller of success in war. Patriotism and duty motivate the people to worship. On sacred days priests, who are state officials, follow prescribed rituals. The people accept the rites without actually being involved. Once a year citizens must worship the emperor by burning incense as an oath of allegiance.

People have the feeling that ritual is more important than their moral and spiritual condition. Prayers are always for an advantage such as safety or health. People even pray for the death of a relative in order to receive the inheritance. If their prayers are unanswered, the people stone, ridicule, and tell ribald jokes about the god. Belief is gone, but the people observe the forms and ceremonies of worship. Recently at the Rostra, a teacher berated the lack of true worship by saying that he wondered how two priests could meet without laughing. Welcome to Rome.

*I am Sulla*, a priestess to the goddess Cybele. The state religion does not satisfy the citizens' spiritual needs. The people have turned to Oriental and Eastern cults that offer emotional involvement. Devotees to Cybele worship her in dance orgies. Others worship Isis through rituals that supposedly lead to immortality. The Mithras cult, which emphasizes high morals, is a strong competitor to a new religion, Christianity. Welcome to Rome.

*I am Julia*, an astrologer. Superstition and fatalism are alive in Rome. Workers of magic, sorcery, and necromancy, diviners of charms and dreams, quacks of every description swarm through the streets. I am a certified astrologer. Citizens consult me daily about how the movement of the stars will affect events in their lives. Many more citizens follow their personal horoscopes. Welcome to Rome.

*I am Luis*, a Jewish rabbi. I live in the main Jewish quarter, Trastevere. Jews have several low-profile synagogues in the city, formed according to professions or interests (for example, lime-kiln workers, cultures, noble patrons, and neighborhoods). One is called "of the Hebrews" because the members still speak the Hebrew language.

Small-time Jewish traders such as match vendors, dealers in second-hand clothes, barters in cookware, money lenders, and rag collectors, are unpopular. The fact that some of our number are honored as senators, doctors, actors, and editors is ignored. The state despises our diligent work, our abstinence of vices, our scorn of their idols, and our refusal to honor their emperor. They even ridicule our physical appearance, our excitable nature, our air of holiness, and our shuffling walk and shabby dress.

The state tolerates our presence by respecting our sabbaths, permitting us to collect and use our own funds, and exempting us from military service. We are citizens with the right to appeal to the emperor. Knowing that we never will be scourged or crucified is a comfort. Yet the Romans fear our frequent complaints, petitions, and easily aroused anger. Recently at the Rostra, an orator lowered his voice at a certain point in his delivery so the Jews would not be alarmed. We are like a grain of sand in their sandals.

Being worshipers of one God, we are considered fanatics. Even so, the Gentile proselytes and God-fearers who have joined our worship confess that Judaism offers hope from the tyranny and evil around us. Our simple services offer an alternative to the sensuous rites of other religions.

News from Jerusalem passes rapidly throughout the towns and cities of the empire. We Jews have debated for the past three years the words and deeds of a man named Jesus from Nazareth in the old country. Lately the activities of Caiaphas, Herod, and Pilate have been the major topics of conversation among the slaves and citizens in the Forum and among the Jews in our shops and hovels. We whisper questions like, "What will the Romans do with a usurper to their power?" and "Will the Roman courts be tolerant with this Jew, Jesus?"

Today the questions were answered. The government news sheet described His crucifixion. Welcome to Rome.

## Something New Comes to Rome

In A.D. 30, many weeks before the Feast of Pentecost, a group of Jews and Jewish converts in Rome decided to attend the feast in Jerusalem. Perhaps they journeyed down the Appian Way to Puteoli, where they boarded a merchant ship bound for Palestine. Disembarking, they followed another Roman road into Jerusalem. On the day of Pentecost, they heard Peter preach.

Returning home, a few miles out on the Appian Way, Rome's skyline came into view. Their steps quickened. They were coming home as a new people with a new message. They went up and down the streets sharing, "Jesus, Lord, Messiah." The idlers, money changers, aristocrats, homemakers, shopkeepers, farmers, slaves, entertainers, Stoics, cultists, Jews, and soldiers repented, received forgiveness and the gift of the Holy Spirit. They became saints in Rome.

For a few years the state tolerated this new group as a sect of Judaism. Under government protection, Christianity spread. Some Romans became Christians after meeting Paul on one of his missionary journeys. Charter members of the church in Rome were strengthened by their reports when they returned home.

Down their own city streets and out onto the roads of the world, Roman Christians witnessed. Paul wrote to them, "Wherever I go I hear you being talked about! For your faith in God is becoming known around the world" (Rom. 1:8 TLB).

# Rome: The Christian Church

Phoebe probably joined a Rome-bound caravan passing through her hometown of Cenchreae, Corinth. Ships regularly left this port for Rome, but women preferred the overland route. Traveling north, they crossed the narrow strait into Italy, then followed the Appian Way into Rome.

Tucked away in Phoebe's satchel was a letter written by Paul to "all God's beloved in Rome" (Rom. 1:7 RSV). The salutation was timeless, and the message as relevant to the twentieth century as to the first. Entrusted to Phoebe was a theological treatise that provided a comprehensive explanation of the gospel. Paul understood the backgrounds of these new Christians in Rome, and he wrote words they could understand.

Roman Christianity grew out of a Jewish background. Therefore, students of the Old Testament listened when Paul wrote that the gospel was announced by the prophets and affirmed by the Law.

Romans were obsessed with power. Their brilliant generals, competent engineers, political geniuses, and power-hungry Caesars romanized an empire. Power-conscious citizens listened when Paul wrote that the gospel, God's power, could transform lives.

Rome was a society where slaves outnumbered citizens. A man in bondage to another listened when Paul referred to himself as a slave of Christ, yet one who possessed complete freedom. In a culture stressing social status, all classes listened when Paul wrote that the gospel was offered freely to everyone. Roman law regulated the minutia of the citizens' lives. In addition, the Jewish community followed rigid rules and imposed their traditions on others. Struggling to reach God through rituals and stifled by rules, folks listened as Paul announced that faith in Christ justifies man before God.

This truth echoed down through the years. One day spiritually troubled Martin Luther understood the significance of Paul's words, "the just shall live by faith" (Rom. 1:17*b* KJV). God's grace as a *gift* became the motivating force in Luther's life. Phoebe carried in her satchel a proclamation that centuries later produced the Protestant Reformation.

Today, when you and I rest secure in our salvation through faith in Christ, when we feel His power surge through our minds and emotions, when we experience freedom in servanthood—we might pause to appreciate the Roman Christians who treasured the letter, the Holy Spirit who protected it through the persecution, and Paul's helper Phoebe.

Paul included in the letter a commendation of Phoebe to the Roman Christians (see Rom. 16:1-2). Such endorsements were necessary because counterfeit believers often took advantage of the Christian community's hospitality. Phoebe, whose name meant "shining one," served the church in Cenchreae. An influential patroness to the oppressed, her life was dedicated to aiding the sick and the poor of the congregation.

## House Church in Rome

Scattered throughout the city, believers met in homes they called house churches. Paul probably never visited a Roman house church, but on his missionary journeys, he made friends with people who now resided in the city. He sent greetings to several whom he mentions in Romans 16.

The Christians who gathered to hear Paul's letter lived with society's precarious tolerance. To the Roman government in the early years, Christianity was only a sect of Judaism. Christians and Jews taught from the same book, and the Christians followed a Jewish leader.

To the pagan citizens, Christians were peculiar because they abstained from banquets and popular amusements.

Believers were unpopular because they insisted on the supremacy of their God, and they honored a Jew who had been crucified as a rebel. Christians were suspected of cannibalism and arson, and had strange ideas, like a disgust for war and a reverence for virginity. To the Jews, Christians were defectors who turned from monotheism to the worship of three Gods.

Those who gathered in the house churches had joined a despised sect, had renounced the state religion, and had endured the pagan society's prejudice. Their responsibility was to declare, "Jesus is Lord" to an imperialistic populace who declared, "Caesar is Lord." However, they were not left to their own resources. The Holy Spirit gave gifts to help them serve each other, glorify God, and live victoriously in their city. Paul discusses the proper use of those gifts in Romans 12:6-8.

Those with the prophetic gift received messages from God dealing with past, present, or future events. The words helped believers cope with their present situation. Prophecies, using only the words inspired by the Spirit, strengthened the church. Uninspired, eloquent speeches simply tickled the ears, as did the philosophers' words at the Forum's Rostra.

Others served faithfully in practical ways behind the scenes. Meaning "personal ministering," the word has the same Greek root as the word *deacon*. As time passed, those who took care of physical needs were called deacons. Servers perceived needs, found resources to meet needs, and ministered wholeheartedly.

Some had the gift of teaching. Gifted teachers shared biblical facts and explained the truth of God's Word so clearly that believers had a foundation for practicing Christian principles.

Some were exhorters. *Exhorter, comforter*, and *advocate* (Latin form) come from the same Greek word meaning "one called alongside to help." An exhorter encouraged, reassured, and steadied those who wavered. On occasion an exhorter urged others to action.

Those with the gift of giving generously ministered through material possessions. The Romans were accustomed to a patron-client relationship. Patrons assumed monetary responsibility for many clients. In return, the clients escorted and supported patrons. However, the doles, or gifts, were given in a condescending manner that made the clients feel inferior. Christians are to give with such cheer or hilarity that those who receive are built up. Gifted givers share with a singleness of mind—without pretense.

Others had the gift to lead. With a genuine, sensitive, servant attitude, they managed with such effectiveness that everyone was blessed. Leaders must exercise the gift with an eager diligence, or the routine matters will become a bore.

In the first century, those with the gift of mercy primarily aided the sick because of the absence of medical facilities or attention. Those with this gift showed compassionate love toward the outcasts, underprivileged, ill, and handicapped. Merciful believers shared themselves with people who could not repay. Often the joyful spirit in which one helped was even more of a blessing than the actual aid.

## Welcome to Your Church

Below are situations that show the parallel between the gifts in the Roman church and in your church. Consider members of your church who exercise the gifts. Affirm them by placing their names in the appropriate blanks. By answering the questions that follow, you may identify whether your gift is included in the Roman list.

•*Prophecy:* The presence of this gift in members motivates involvement in social and moral issues affecting the community. They often endure criticism for taking a stand for justice and righteousness. The gift is not limited to public life. In a prayer service, a person gifted with prophecy may share a testimony, and the words directly enter the heart of a listener who is then encouraged and comforted. Though the one with this gift has an aura of authority, the gift is used in faith, not in a self-confident spirit.

I affirm _____'s gift of prophesy. Do you speak words that challenge people to change?

• *Service*: Gifted servers form the backbone of the body. They volunteer for the unseen jobs, but their work strengthens others.

Early one Saturday morning, while I arranged a conference room, I noticed energetic activity around me. Repair persons painted, glued, moved furniture, tacked carpet, and tightened hinges. I mentioned the busyness to the staff person who assisted me. He explained that a few years before, the church needed minor repairs. When the pastor called for help from the members, these men and women volunteered. Experiencing such pleasure on that first Saturday, the volunteers continued to spend a part of every Saturday staying ahead of major maintenance problems. The staff person added, "Visitors and members comment about the neatness and beauty of the buildings. But probably very few know what goes on here most Saturdays." The Saturday crew had been regular attenders at the Sunday morning services, but they had never been participators until the church tapped their gifts of service.

The gifts of service and helping overlap under the umbrella of ministry. A fine distinction between the two is that those gifted with service are more task-oriented, like the repair persons. Those gifted with helps are more people-oriented. They enjoy activities such as hosting fellowships, or shopping for the disabled.

As I was writing this chapter my neighbor, Norman, asked me for a key to unlock our church. He said, "I've noticed a loose hymnal rack on a pew. I can tighten it." The Normans in our churches are like oil that soothe the other parts.

I affirm _____'s gift of service.
Do you enjoy doing the "thankless" jobs?

•*Teaching:* Gifted teachers have keen interest in disciplined study. Then they share the information in simple ways that cause members to say, "I understand." To communicate the Scriptures, the teaching gift is used in a variety of settings such as the classroom, pulpit, media, drama, or music.

Our church's minister of music is a Bible teacher. Allow me to explain. Our choir prepares the congregation for worship. The ladies ensemble  elicits tears of joy. The men's quartet prompts "amens" and patting feet. Every solo lifts our spirits. The instrumentalists lead worshipers in soul searching. The director selects music with biblically based content. We worshipers hear the voices and the melodies, but the message pricks the mind and stimulates us to say, "I see. I understand more of God's Word to me."

I affirm _____'s gift of teaching.
Do people thank you for presenting the gospel in a way that is understandable?

•<u>Exhortation</u>: A gifted exhorter is the one to whom you turn when you have an aching heart or troubled emotions. She or he encourages you to feel special, and challenges you to say, "I can do that!" Gifted exhorters walk among us with a sensitivity to all that is happening. When they see someone falter, they extend a steadying hand. The private incident is known only to the stumbler and the exhorter. Sometimes the exhorter must speak words of warning or admonition. Members heed the reproof because they know the words are spoken with love and concern for the body.

I affirm _____'s gift of exhortation.
Do you encourage and comfort strugglers?

•*Giving:* Gifted givers have the ability to make money and use it to bless, *not* control, a church. However, gifted givers are not limited to those who are financially comfortable or wealthy.

Mrs. Combs, a gifted giver, was a member of our first church. Instead of an overabundance of material possessions, she possessed a green thumb and a fertile garden plot. Something grew in her garden every month of the year except January.

One morning I responded to Mrs. Comb's invitation to "drop by the house." She motioned for me to back up the car to the porch, then she proceeded to load the trunk with boxes of canned fruit and vegetables. To a city gal who did not know that English peas grew anywhere except in a can, I was overwhelmed. Delightfully stunned, I lent a hand and listened to her explanation.

"I can't give much money to our church, but I can help by giving food to our pastor's family. I decided to tithe my canning jars. Every tenth jar I set aside for you."

For eight years, I eagerly responded to Mrs. Comb's frequent invitation to "drop by the house today." Her cheerful, liberal gift blessed and strengthened me. The memory of it still does!

I affirm _____'s gift of giving.
Do you give to the church sacrificially and without boasting?
Do you ask, "How much can I give?" rather than "How much can I keep?"

•*Leading:* A gifted leader is an efficient, prompt, no-excuses person. Relaxed in knowing what has to be done to achieve certain goals for a meeting, program, or emphasis, the leader delegates responsibility. Allowing the Lord to direct, a gifted leader does not walk far ahead of the volunteers he or she leads.

Often people without the gift of leading occupy leadership positions. The ungifted leader can easily become domineering, not serving; dictatorial, not humble; opinionated, not receptive; insensitive, not tactful; manipulating, not ministering. The diligent leader follows the admonition of Peter to lead by a good example, not by domination (see 1 Peter 5:3).

I affirm _____'s gift of leadership.

Do you easily delegate responsibility?

Do you like to set goals and discover the best ways to reach them?

•*Mercy:* Those gifted with mercy willingly help the type of people described in Matthew 25:35-36. They balance empathy and objectivity. They do not become so burdened that they lose sight of the helping alternatives. Sometimes speaking is inappropriate in a ministering situation. The merciful sit silently beside a hurting person without feeling threatened. The merciful find fulfillment in sharing their time, privacy, and patience with suffering people. They live caring life-styles and greet every opportunity to relieve pain with cheerfulness.

The merciful act out good intentions. They do not say, "If I can do anything, call me." They fluff the pillows, scrub the bathroom, or baby sit. I read about a church that functions around the members' gifts. Those who had the gift of mercy mobilized their gifts for service. They provided Sunday School classes for various kinds of handicapped people.

I affirm _____'s gift of mercy.

Do you enjoy giving hope to those in need?

## The Body: Yielded for Service
## (Rom. 12:1-2)

*Body* was an unusually important word in Roman society. Roman culture, permeated by Greek thought, stressed the imprisoned soul's desire to free itself from the body, either through a life of self-denial, or through fleshly indulgences. In contrast, the Incarnation showed God's acceptance of the human body as it became the sanctuary for His Spirit.

Using "altar" language, Paul pleads for Christians, in remembrance of and gratitude for God's mercies (see Rom. 1-11), to surrender their bodies to God. He calls for voluntary commitment of the total self to a life of service in the temporal world. Because of the Holy Spirit within us, the sacrifice is in living, in contrast to the death of slain animals in the Jewish rituals and pagan cult rites. Because of the Spirit within, the sacrifice is holy and cleansed. Just as blemished animals were unacceptable in the Jewish sacrifices, stained lives cannot be surrendered in service to God.

As a child, worship to me meant pews and preachers, prayers and pretty windows. Corporate worship is good and necessary. However, the personal dedication of self, available to be like Jesus in the ordinary experiences of daily life, is the highest worship.

We are to live like butterflies in a grubby world. The transformation from the old life to the new is as miraculous as the metamorphosis of the worm into a graceful winged delight. The change is perfected through the mind—all that is our conscious self. The renewed mind is bent on finding the will of God, and discovers through actual experience that His will is good (not in error), acceptable (worthy), and perfect (accomplishes its purpose).

## The Body: Yielded Through Service (Rom. 12:3-6*a*)

Paul introduced the use of gifts by reminding his readers that the many members of our human body constitute a unity. In the human body, one member cannot perform all the functions.

In the same way, spiritually we are one body in Christ.

"In Christ" does not refer to each believer's relationship to Christ, as Paul describes in Romans 6:11. In this passage, Paul indicates that our individual union "in Christ" makes us belong to one another. By serving Christ with our gifts, we serve one another. In like manner, by serving one another, we serve Christ. The Scriptures never speak of church members nor of membership in local congregations; the Scriptures always refer to membership in the body of Christ. We are one by the Spirit, not by any human action.

In the body of Christ, one richly endowed believer cannot be and do everything. All members, harmonizing a diversity of impressive or inconspicuous gifts, cause the body to function properly. An attempt to stereotype members of the body conflicts with the good, acceptable, perfect will of God.

In the human body, one member does not receive praise to the exclusion of the others. An orator's total self is honored, not just his mouth. If a finger touches a live wire, the whole body is shocked. In the body of Christ, when your gift edifies, all members benefit, and God is glorified. If a member abuses a gift, all suffer and God is dishonored.

In the human body, limbs and organs do not envy or argue about their importance. The humble and the prominent parts alike function for the good of the whole. In the body of Christ, members envy, bicker, or feel superior because of a tendency to overestimate the importance of particular gifts.

An undercurrent of superiority permeated Rome's secular society. Evidently new Christians with this haughty attitude threatened the unity of the body. So Paul commanded, "Do not think of yourself more highly than you should" (v. 3).

The yielded life includes total commitment of our gifts. Between the extremes of false humility and arrogant airs is a place for an honest assessment of those gifts. Appreciation of the interdependence of our gifts suppresses pride. On the altar of self-sacrifice, we recognize that we are members of the body because of God's mercy.

## The Body: Yielded in Love
## (Rom. 12:9-21)

A yielded life, nurtured in the fellowship of believers, will translate God's mercies into practical living. Paul did not define love, but he described how love talks and walks—how Jesus would behave if He physically lived among us. At the foot of Ann Street Hill, I became His follower, and He became my example. In your special place where you accepted Christ as Saviour, He became incarnate in your life, too. Using our gifts, we behave like Him.

After reading Romans 12:9-21, ask yourself, "Do I have an accurate evaluation of self that will cause me to value others? Do I substitute sentimentalism or a patronizing pat for Christlike love? Is there a conflict between my belief and my behavior?" In these verses, Paul describes Christlike love in the following ways:

• *Love is sincere.* In Greek drama the actors, or *hypocrites*, carried masks to distinguish between tragic and comic characters. They faked their feelings. The Roman Christians understood that pretending to love was as superficial as changing masks.

• *Genuine love truly hates evil.* Some people avoid trouble for fear of the results. Others desire the good but will be content with the status quo. Love tries to eliminate evil, and to make the good better.

• *Love respects.* Instead of honoring others, self-advancement at any cost was common in Rome. The church, Christ's body, demonstrated love as members shared burdens, and as they edified and honored one another.

• *Love works.* Love "boils" and glows with enthusiastic fervor for serving the Lord as a bondslave serves his master. Laziness is unacceptable behavior in the life of a Christian.

• *Love endures.* Christians possess optimism and hope that inspires endurance through frustration, and enables them to meet tragedy with a victorious tenacity. The Roman Christians were surrounded by Stoics who faced life's heartaches with a stiff upper lip. But distressed Christians do not have to pretend boldness. Even in sorrow, there is joy in the confidence that God controls the circumstances. Perseverance in prayer supports love that overcomes the pressures of a hostile world.

• *Love gives.* Some religionists give alms to the poor in order to acquire merit. However, Christians give because of a sincere concern for people. Stewards recognize that all possessions are the Lord's; we manage them until He directs how they are to be shared.

• *Love expresses hospitality.* Because the inns in Rome were uncomfortable and dangerous, Christians opened their homes to travelers. More than entertaining strangers, we are to pursue others with our hospitality and kindness.

• *Love forgives.* When people hurt us, our old nature wants to retaliate, which increases the strain. The surrendered saint, forgiving those who cause hurt, reflects the attitude of Jesus (see Matt. 5:44; Luke 6:28). Like loving, blessing those who injure or insult us requires sincerity. Speaking in silver tones while seething inside is like wearing two masks.

Even though our goal is to live in peace, sometimes attempts to make peace fail. On occasion our words or intentions are misinterpreted. Even in apparent failure in reconciliation, God does not withhold His peace from us. Christianity is not an easy going acceptance of all issues in order to avoid a clash. Battles may be necessary to keep us from compromising principles.

Faced by hurts, our old nature wants revenge. No human possesses the knowledge required to judge others' motives or actions. Only God, Who knows the situation, can administer justice in love. Personal retaliation indicates a lack of confidence in God to take care of us.

On the other hand, we might be tempted to taunt, "I can't get even, but God will give you what you deserve." Refraining from revenge is not enough; we must actively show love to an enemy. The Romans were familiar with the sight of Egyptians balancing vessels of burning charcoal on their heads to show penance. Because the enemy expects hate, undeserved kindness will make an impression, causing a sense of burning shame, like coals on the enemy's head, which might lead to repentance.

• *Love laughs and cries.* Stoics taught that a good life depended on an impassive detachment for persons and things. Christians in their love-motivated life show happiness for a friend's good fortune and sadness for another's misfortune. Unfeigned love rejoices and grieves. In fact, tears form the strongest bonds between two people.

The story is told of Sadie, a beloved nannie, who returned from the funeral of a fellow slave. The mistress of the plantation embraced her and sympathized, "Dear Sadie, I'm so sorry. You and Daisy were such close friends."

"Just 'quaintances," sighed Sadie.

"Nannie Sadie, what do you mean, 'just acquaintances'? You and Daisy worked and lived together for 40 years."

"Yes, but we never cried together."

# Ephesus: The City

From the West traders, tourists, and travelers on ships in the Aegean Sea strained for a glimpse of Ephesus, the "light of Asia." Some distance from the harbor, the towering marble temple to Diana (Artemis) glistened like an ornament. No wonder poets compared the temple to the wonders of Babylon and the pyramids in Egypt. Mount Prion and Mount Corsessus, covered with lush vineyards, formed valleys that cupped the city. While navigating the narrow, three-mile Cayster River to the harbor, visitors had their first view of the marble Great Theater, located at the junction of the two major city streets. Since Ephesus was on the main sea route from Rome to Asia, the harbor was always jammed with an international crowd, and was crammed with imported merchandise.

From the East, a steady flow of folks followed the Roman roads of Asia Minor that intersected in Ephesus. Winding their way down the mountains the traders, tourists, and travelers from the interior of Asia entered the city through the arched Magnesian Gate. In the distance the sixty foot high columns of the temple of Diana cast long shadows down the slopes.

In the valley below, Ephesus twinkled like a precious gem. The sight of the white marble structures, overlaid with gold and decorated with brightly painted frescoes, generated gasps of excitement among the walkers. Hurrying past the suburban, multi-storied residences of the wealthy, and the small Odeion theater, they joined the noisy confusion at the intersection of the Arcadia Way and Harbor Street in front of the Great Theater. There, in the center of the city, the trap slammed shut. Ephesus, appearing so pure, clean, and beautiful from the harbor and the hill, boiled like a caldron of evil.

A few of the 250,000 Ephesian citizens will describe life in the most influential city of the Roman Province of Asia. *I am Elise*, a tour guide. Since tourism is the city's major industry, we residents welcome the big spenders. I guide tourists to the attractions that lured them our way. Our present city is relatively new. Tiberus rebuilt it in A.D. 29 following an earthquake. Settled by Greek colonists, the personality of Ephesus resembles Corinth more than Rome.

When visitors debark at the harbor, they follow the Arcadia Way to the center of town. The marble street is 1,740 feet long, and so wide that eight chariots can ride side by side. The gates at each end of the Arcadia Way are two of our oldest monuments. Former slaves, Mazeus and Mithridates, built them in 4 B.C. to honor Agrippa, Augustus' son-in law, who arranged their freedom. One of our city's favorite historical stories is about a parade on the Arcadia Way to celebrate the visit of Anthony and Cleopatra. The excitement ceased when our forefathers learned the couple had come to borrow money.

The Arcadia Way intersects with Harbor Street near the Great Theater. Porticoes, monuments, fountains, and marble benches line both streets. The brothels, public baths, and Roman lavatories comprise downtown Ephesus. Across from the brothels and enclosed by a colonnaded walkway is the Lower Agora (mall) or commercial center. Souvenir vendors, tent makers, traders, and bakers prosper alongside sculptors, painters, architects and builders. One of the benefits of working in the Agora is a five-hour midday siesta.

The Library of Celsus is a prestigious landmark in the Lower Agora. The two story building houses 9,500 scrolls. The Street of Curetes connects the Lower Agora to the Upper Agora, the administrative center. A large stadium and several temples complete the downtown complex. In addition to the temple of Diana, many other temples and shrines dot the city. The shrines to Isis and Serapis are important to the many Egyptian sailors and merchants. Trying to recruit mercenaries for their army, the Egyptians are a constant presence in our city. Also, Jews worship in several synagogues. We Ephesians tolerate many religions as long as tourism, trade, and the worship of Diana thrive.

When you return home, help us advertise. Tell your friends about Ephesus' mild climate and pure air. Talk about our amiable, elegantly dressed citizens with refined manners. Brag about the glorious pomp of our deity Diana's worship.

Great is Diana of Ephesus. Welcome!

*I am Uel*, the city clerk. I am the most important political figure in the city. I preside at meetings, draft decrees, and seal them with the public seal. The city clerk position is rotated among leading citizens.

My office is located in the Upper Agora, the administrative center for the province. The town hall, the stock exchange, and the school of Tyrannus are across the court. In the Upper Agora, we entertain dignitaries at state functions and listen to politicians debate, philosophers teach, and poets read. From the Upper Agora, I view the bustling activity of our city. No wonder the bee, stamped on our coins, is the city's emblem.

My major worry is keeping the peace. Recently the silversmiths reacted violently to the preaching of a man named Paul. They rallied at the Great Theater and accused him of undermining their business and of renouncing Diana. Their accusations nearly caused a riot. Finally I intervened, reminding them that their irresponsible action jeopardized the city. We could lose our autonomy. Local officials must maintain order or Rome will take away our freedom.

Great is Diana of Ephesus. Welcome!

*I am Theon*, an Asiarch, or one of the provincial officers. Since the Roman governor resides in Ephesus instead of Pergamum, the capital city, the province's business transpires in the Upper Agora. Provincial officers, sometime called chiefs of Asia, are chosen from important families. I am responsible for emperor worship in several cities and assist the priests in the temple rites. From my own estate, I sponsor games and celebrations connected with emperor worship.

My friend Uel, the city clerk, mentioned the tent maker/preacher Paul. When I met him, I immediately liked his openness and enthusiasm for his beliefs. I felt like he would want to defend himself before the silversmiths; I sent him word not to get involved in the mob scene.

Great is Diana of Ephesus. Welcome!

*I am Irenaeus*, a priest in the temple of Diana, a fertility goddess. Hundreds of priests, eunuchs, and temple prostitutes who staff the temple live in cells within the temple compound.

The temple, an imposing white, blue, red, and yellow marble structure, dominates the skyline. Architects erected the temple on marshland to avoid earthquake damage. Built on a high platform, the temple's 127 Ionic columns span an area 425 feet long and 200 feet wide. Life-size statues decorate the base of the columns. The roof is made of white marble tiles. Behind the altar is the mummified, many-breasted image of Diana. In the center of the altar area is the sacred stone, thrown from heaven by Zeus. (The stone is probably a meteorite which supposedly resembles Diana.) The Ephesians boast of being the guardians of Zeus' gift, and of Diana.

Since Diana is considered the deity for the whole province of Asia, devotees from every province contributed to the temple's building cost and maintenance. The temple is a museum where priceless paintings and statues are preserved. The monetary generosity of the worshipers enable the priests, who act as bankers, to buy valuable land and control the fisheries. The Temple treasury is the bank for Asia Minor. Kings, cities, and wealthy citizens deposit money for safe-keeping. Other treasures are stored in the temple's secret chambers.

Great is Diana of Ephesus. Welcome!

*I am Rhea*, a priestess dedicated to prostitution in the

temple of Diana. Priestesses, who are also called "bees," guide devotees in the religious orgies. During Artemision (March and April), our sacred months, I organize festivals, including athletic events, dramatic presentations, and musical contests.

Great is Diana of Ephesus. Welcome!

*I am Hera*, a thief. Other criminals and I live in a tent village surrounding the temple of Diana. We cannot be arrested within a bow shot of the temple. Great is Diana of Ephesus who protects criminals and encourages crime. Welcome!

*I am Krono*, a Greek actor. I moved to Ephesus because of the extraordinary Great Theater, in which the best Greek drama is performed. Located in the center of town, the semicircular theater is 495 feet in diameter, and will seat 25,000 people. The 22 foot wide stage has a scene building (like a wall at the rear of the stage) with seven windows. The purpose of the windows is to present scenery for the acts in the dramas. Since most stages have only three to five windows, the Ephesus stage offers variety in scene presentations. Odeion, a smaller theater used for poet readings, lectures, and concerts, will seat 1,400 people.

Great is Diana of Ephesus. Welcome!

*I am Papias*, owner of a bakery in the Lower Agora. I am a concessionaire, which means the city leaders gave special permission for me to open the bakery. Because of our union's recent protest in a labor dispute, the authorities accused us of "unrestrained evil speaking" and called us a "seditious group of bakers in the marketplace." The city clerk reproved us with an edict which read in part, "I therefore order the Bakers' Union not to hold meetings as a faction, nor to be leaders in recklessness, but strictly to obey the regulations made for the general welfare and to supply the city unfailingly with the labour essential for bread-making."

Great is Diana of Ephesus. Welcome!

*I am Ares*, a trader in the Lower Agora. Ephesian traders

are known over the world as dealers in gold, silver, jewelry, and valuable slaves. I specialize in selling red lead mined in the nearby quarries. Next door, my friend sells a variety of dyes and salves. Up the way is a honey vendor and at the end of the colonnade is a tent making business. Great is Diana of Ephesus. Welcome!

*I am Demetrius*, a silversmith and owner of one of the many successful souvenir shops. All of the thousands of tourists who come to worship Diana buy souvenirs as mementos of their visit. We manufacture miniature temples, shrines, and images of the sacred stone. We also sell terra cotta and marble replicas. This season the most popular souvenir is a small clay female figure set in a shell. Buyers choose between the figure holding a tambourine or a cup, or with a lion seated at her side or beneath her feet. Tourists usually bury these items in the graves with their loved ones. We don't care what they do with the replicas. Our purpose is to increase funds for the temple treasury.

United in a guild, silversmiths control the sale of the souvenirs. Our business is expanding. The crowds create such a demand for these mementos that many craftsmen, including designers, molders, engravers, and jewelers are employed to manufacture the images. Most of the skilled workers are slaves from Rome's military conquests. Great is Diana of Ephesus. Welcome!

*I am Euse,* a magician. The worship of Diana fosters fear of the unknown and mysterious. Magicians, exorcists, and healers sell amulets, charms, and books on magical arts called "Ephesian Letters," to the tourists. They buy the items to ensure fertility, for success in business undertakings, and as remedies for sickness. People think the items bring good fortune. Great is Diana of Ephesus. Welcome!

*I am Menides*, one of the ten priests in the emperor's temple. I lead the people in emperor worship. A frieze showing sacrificial animals and military weapons stands in front of the temple. Some worshipers in other parts of Asia mark their foreheads and hands with a tatoo of the emperor, which allows them to buy food in the marketplace.

Great is Diana of Ephesus. Welcome!

The residents and tourists stumbled along through a dark life, pursuing meaningless goals. Refusing to accept any knowledge of God, their minds were empty. Their hearts were insensitive, cold, and hard like the marble in their buildings. Abandoning themselves to vile conduct, they lost their sense of decency and shame.

Paul walked into this sordid center of paganism on his third missionary journey. For three years he preached, taught, and  performed miracles. As a result of his ministry, souvenir shops closed, innkeepers latched their doors, priests' and priestesses' services declined, bank incomes decreased, exorcist activity dwindled, craftsmen sat idle, practitioners of magic burned the formulas and books, and converted tourists went home, never again to walk the Ephesus way.

What happened? Paul taught that gods made with hands are not God (see Acts 19:24-27), and he proclaimed Jesus as Lord. Many pagans became gifted babes in Christ. Joined to His body, they became the church in Ephesus. Up and down their city streets, they shared "Jesus, Lord" to a sinister populace who shouted, "Great is Diana of Ephesus." Compelled to minister through a variety of gifts, the new Christians changed their city. The power of the gospel undermined the pagan religion that fed the economy and determined the life-style of people.

When Paul walked out of the city of Ephesus, he said good-bye to new saints in the body of Christ.

# Ephesus: The Christian Church

Paul left Ephesus, but he did not forget the new Christians. While imprisoned in Rome, Paul wrote a letter to be circulated among the churches in Asia Minor. We know the letter as the book of Ephesians. The non-controversial message of Ephesians was not directed to a specific problem. Rather, it developed the concept of Christ's sufficiency. Chapters 1-3 assure us that disunity in the universe will harmonize when all people and all things are reconciled in Christ. Chapters 4-6 explain the church's function in achieving the unity.

We who are members of the body are Christ's partners in reconciling the world. The Lord seeks helpers who are rooted and grounded in love. He also seeks those who possess certain qualities.

First, humility, a trait despised in Ephesus, was exalted when Jesus voluntarily became a man. Humble people accept themselves and recognize the worth of others. A second trait, gentleness, means controlled power like that found in a tamed race horse. A gentle person's total personality, expressed through thoughts, words, and actions, are God-controlled. Third, patience is the ability to endure disappointments, to bear another's weaknesses without complaint, and to be gracious toward unpleasant people. Fourth, forbearance is a mutual attitude of understanding between people. Love that wills the highest good for one another binds together these qualities, forming the foundation of our Christian unity.

The oneness of the body is a reality. We refer to "church splits" among members of the visible body. However, the body of Christ is as indestructible as the unity of the Trinity. One Spirit creates and animates the one body. One

Lord is the center of our trust and our expectancy of a heavenly home. One God creates, controls, and sustains one family. We must expend all of our physical and mental energies to preserve the unity. This unity is not an external, uniform organization; it is a heart unity, blending relationships and attitudes without diminishing individuality.

Just as Paul taught the Corinthians and Romans, he reminds the Ephesians that the unity of the body is not characterized by uniformity, but by an exciting diversity of gifted people (see Eph. 4:7). In 1 Corinthians 12 and Romans 12, Paul lists some of the gifts given by the Holy Spirit. In Ephesians 4:11, he refers to leaders, gifted by Christ, who will maintain the mission of the church.

Apostles spoke with authority on matters of faith and practice because they had been with the Lord from His baptism to His resurrection. These traveling messengers were sent out for the special purpose of laying the foundation of the church. In 2 Corinthians 8:23, the word *messenger* is the Greek word for "apostle." Paul referred to leaders commissioned by the church to do a missions task.

Believers in Ephesus did not have Bibles as we have today. Since the church cannot exist apart from God's Word, the Holy Spirit shared God's truths with the prophets. They stood before the people, proclaimed God's message, interpreted revelations, and urged people to respond. God gave direction to His people through the prophets.

Evangelists, or itinerant preachers, had a consuming passion for the unsaved. They communicated the gospel with unusual clarity, and called for decisions. These evangelists expanded the church throughout the provincial centers of Asia Minor.

The pastor/teacher, who had a more settled ministry than the apostles, prophets, or evangelists, possessed one gift with two distinct ministries. Pastor means "to shepherd," implying the giving of spiritual leadership by feeding, protecting, and warning. The pastor was also the church's primary teacher. Relapsing into paganism was a constant danger for members in the first century churches. Teachers had the solemn duty of filling the dark minds of these new Christians with enlightening truths about God. Teachers were entrusted with the task of verbally telling the story of Jesus and explaining Christian doctrines.

According to Ephesians 4:12, these leaders did not monopolize the church's ministry. They prepared all members to perform their individual ministries. Leaders who teach the Word are equipping and developing members to be participators, not spectators, in building up the body. Paul used a medical term to explain the leaders' responsibilities. *Perfecting* means "to set a bone." The function of a leader is "to see that the members of the church are so educated, so helped, so guided, so cared for, so sought after when they go astray, that they become what they ought to be."

The emphasis is on the entire fellowship, striving to be a mature congregation. The leaders create an atmosphere in which members can grow in their trust, obedience, and understanding of Christ. Spiritual maturity becomes evident in at least four ways:

• through a clear reflection of Jesus in believers' lives.
• through stability demonstrated by not following the newest religious fads or doctrines devised by clever speakers.
• through speaking the truth in love. Accurate statements spoken in superior tones or in a harsh manner offend. Truth should be stated with a sincere desire to edify.
• through cooperation.

## Welcome to Your Church

The following suggestions show the responsibility of gifted leadership described by Paul in his letter to the church at Ephesus. Consider your church leaders who exhibit the gifts. Affirm them by placing their names in the blanks. Answering the questions will encourage you in the use of your gift, help you identify your gift, or aid in understanding God's call to a church related vocation.

• *Apostle:* As stated earlier, this office ceased in a restricted sense with the death of the original apostles. The foundation of the church was in place. Still, in a broad sense, this gift applies to every Christian who heeds the commission, "As the Father sent me, so I send you." The apostolic gift is evident in missionaries who cross cultural barriers.

I affirm _____'s ability to adapt to change.

Are you willing to volunteer to use your gift to help a missionary on a home or foreign missions field?

• *Prophets*: Prophets today do not speak forth new truths. Rather, they give members a clearer understanding of the changeless revelations in the Scriptures. In a new mission or Bible fellowship, the prophet's gift gives direction for the discipline and functions of the work.

I affirm _____'s gift of prophecy.

Do you have the ability to reveal God's truth to others?

• *Evangelist:* When an evangelist proclaims the gospel, members experience fresh enthusiasm to continue in their spiritual growth. The evangelist moves on, but leaves a renewed sense of power among the members. Some people are uniquely gifted to present the gospel to large groups of people. However, all of us have the privilege of sharing Christ by our personal testimony. Every day the Lord places people in our paths who need to hear about Jesus with simplicity and with compassion.

I affirm _____'s gift of evangelism.

Do you direct conversations toward witnessing opportunities?

Are you comfortable in sharing your testimony with nonbelievers?

• *Pastor/Teacher:* A gifted pastor/teacher, the overseer of the local body of believers, introduces new believers to the Christian life and helps them mature in their faith. In the shepherd role, the pastor feeds the flock from God's Word, strengthens believers through their struggles, and shares their sorrows and joys. Neither knowledge gained by an accumulation of degrees nor ignorance from an aversion to formal study will make a person a pastor. Christ Himself gives the shepherd heart—a yearning to bring lost people into a safe fold. In the teacher role, this leader reminds the sheep of a neglected truth and inspires them to search the Scriptures.

Are your church leaders training the members to exercise their gifts? Is your congregation composed of spectators who insist that the paid staff do all the ministering and witnessing?

I affirm _____'s gift as pastor/teacher.

Do you like to take responsibility for helping others grow spiritually?

Do you attempt to cultivate friendships with people and make them feel comfortable in your church?

## The Body: Healthy and Growing (Eph. 4:15*b*-16)

For the Ephesian church, Paul's emphasis was on the growth of the body rather than comparison of the human anatomy to the members of Christ's body. In the human body the head, sending impulses and messages to all the parts, controls life processes. All body parts depend on the brain for the important functions of life. As the Head of His body, the church, Christ nourishes and energizes the gifts of every member. Under Christ's control the members:

• harmonize and unite their gifts.

• minister to and feel connected with each other. The word *joint* means "fastens or binds together different parts of the frame; such as blood vessels, tendons, muscles." The human body grows as each part nourishes other parts. In the church, God's strength flows through your gift into me and from my gift into you. We all benefit from each other, and together build up the body. Christ fastens together all the parts to form a living organism.

• contribute to the growth of the whole body. No member should be idle or overworked. A church grows in proportion to the proper functioning of the gifts in individual members.

## Behavior Necessary for Body Unity (Eph. 4:25-32)

Paul couched the description of gifted leadership between the moral qualities and the behavior of believers necessary for body unity. Behavior that was acceptable in Ephesus and in our twentieth century society is condemned by Christianity, and is undesirable for members of the body. Paul exhorts us to make our behavior consistent with our beliefs. To discontinue negative conduct or disposition is not enough. These must be replaced with positive actions and attitudes. For example:

• Do not lie; do be truthful. Members of our physical body do not lie to each other. Chrysostom, one of the fathers of the early church, wrote an absurd analogy about the eye and foot lying to each other: "Let not the eye lie to the foot, nor the foot to the eye. If there be a deep pit and its mouth covered with reeds shall present to the eye the appearance of solid ground, will not the eye use the foot to ascertain whether it is hollow underneath, or whether it is firm and resists? Will the foot tell a lie, and not the truth as it is? And what, again, if the eye were to spy a serpent or a wild beast, will it lie to the foot?" Believers must be reliable in their contacts with everyone. Fellowship must be built on trust; lies threaten the unity of a church.

• Do not lose your temper; do be angry against injustices. However, even righteous indignation can degenerate into resentment. Denunciation of sin must be done with tenderness. Anger harms when it arises from injured pride,

malice, or desire for revenge. Uncontrolled anger deterio-
rates relationships and the dissension gives the devil an
opportunity to fan the flame.
• Do not steal; do labor honestly to support self and to
give to those in need.
• Do not speak evil; do speak constructively. Evil is a
word used for rotten fruit. It applies to obscene, unkind, or
untrue talk that hurts the hearer. Unsavory talk also
grieves the Holy Spirit Who resides in us.
• Do not hold grudges, feel hostility, quarrel, defame rep-
utations, or harbor ill will; do imitate God by being forgiving, kind, and loving. Sacrificial love for others becomes a
fragrant offering acceptable to God. The saints in Ephesus
walked in love. The aggressive use of their gifts was a witness to all of Asia.

## A Postscript and a Warning

Years passed. The Ephesians received another letter.
Through the pen of John, the risen Lord spoke: "I know
your works, your labor, your patience" (Rev. 2:2 author's
paraphrase). After the commendation, He added, "But
you have left your first love" (v. 4). First love is consuming, unselfish, and fervent.

Writing to the Thessalonians, Paul commended them
for actions that demonstrated a consuming, unselfish, and
fervent love: "Remembering without ceasing your work of
faith, and labour of love, and patience of hope in our Lord
Jesus Christ" (1 Thess. 1:3 KJV). The churches were similar,
yet the Ephesians lacked three qualities: faith, hope, and
love. When love leaves, faith and hope follow. Only the
externals of religious activity remain: perfectly implement-
ed programs; determination without compassion to minister; and orthodox worship services. The use of gifts motivated by human might, not by the Spirit, spawns ceaseless
activity. Busyness does not necessarily give light to the
world. The warning is that, unless we love, the Lord will
remove His presence.

The risen Lord is trustworthy.

# The Provinces of Asia Minor: Pontus, Galatia, Cappadocia, Asia, Bithynia

I stood in awe before the papal altar in Saint Peter's Basilica, Vatican City. Uniquely proportioned for the 150-foot-high domed ceiling, the altar dominates the nave. The colossal, cross-shaped church, capable of seating more than 50,000, marks the tomb of Simon Peter, referred to as *saint* in those environs.

A walk through the enormous vastness of the cathedral, adorned with the masterpieces of artistic geniuses, is a sensory experience. The beauty touches a manifold (to borrow a word from Peter) of emotions. The bold baroque sculpture of Bernini contrasts with the exquisite elegance of Michelangelo's chiseled human-like figures.

Seated against one of the plastered walls is a statue of Peter. Since the thirteenth century, worshipers have venerated the image. The toe on the right foot of the statue is worn away by the kisses of millions of faithful pilgrims. For a long time, I gazed as hundreds of people genuflected, caressed the garment, and kissed his foot. In his youthful years the overconfident, presumptuous Peter might have been flattered by such a grand memorial.

"This is not the Peter I know," I whispered. The Peter I know had a problem with his feet; he balked when Jesus knelt to bathe them. The pivotal foot washing experience prompted him to write in later years, "Clothe yourself with humility toward one another, for God is opposed to the proud, but gives grace to the humble" (1 Peter 5:5*b* NASB). Humbled Peter served as a shepherd to the flock—quite a contrast to the trappings in the magnificent mausoleum dedicated to his honor.

## Asia Minor

The people to whom Peter wrote lived in the interior of Asia Minor, in the provinces of Pontus, Galatia, Cappadocia, and Asia. Paul visited some of the cities in Galatia and Asia on his missionary journeys, and John wrote to seven churches in Asia. Peter's letter addressed the problems of harassed Christians who lived out of the mainstream traffic of major cities. Let's meet a few of those people.

*I am Lucretia*, from the province of Pontus. Settled by Greek colonists, Pontus is also the administrative center for the province of Bithynia. Our beautiful walled city, located on the Black Sea, is the envy of Asia Minor. We are especially proud of our ornately decorated public buildings. The city of Trapezue, also on the Black Sea, is the port of supply for Roman armies on the frontier.

My husband is part owner of the local ship-building industry. Our ships are exported all over the world. In the fertile valleys of the mountains farmers produce olives and grains, and raise sheep. The mountains, by the way, are covered with beech, pine, and oak forests.

Rumors accuse Nero of setting fire to Rome in order to rebuild the city to suit his extravagant tastes. Though the city is many miles away from us, our miners are benefiting from the fire. They work overtime filling Nero's demands for iron, copper, and silver.

My family enjoys an affluent life-style. I can afford fashionable clothes and jewelry, and one of my favorite pastimes is experimenting with hairstyles.

Aquila and Priscilla, a local couple who make tents and travel a lot, told me about the Lord. I accepted Christ as Saviour, but my husband still worships at the shrine of MA. Living for Christ in my home is difficult. I am sometimes tempted to renounce Christianity and return to paganism. Recently my sister Maria, also a Christian, died. We believers celebrated the end of her sojourn here on earth and rejoiced in the heavenly reunion with her husband Daniel. Their tombstones, standing among the graves of the deceased who worshiped MA, are testimonies to their faith. They read: "Here lies a servant of God, Daniel," and "Here lies the handmaid of God, Maria."

The Jews in the local synagogue constantly nag the Roman officials, claiming that we Christians are separate from the Jewish community. They urge the government to ban us as illegal residents. So far, the government has ignored the Jews' request. Roman thought is, "Why bother with a few people who follow a dead hero?" Welcome to Pontus.

*I am Marcus*, proconsul, or chief, of Asia. I live in Tavium, one of the three major cities in the province of Galatia. Each city annually appoints a delegate to the provincial council. As a civil official with a few priestly duties, my main responsibility is to conduct festivals to honor the emperor. I spend several weeks of the year in Ephesus representing my area of Galatia in the administrative Agora.

Our province, 175 miles wide and 250 miles long, sprawls across the middle of Asia Minor. I act as deputy for a variety of people. The larger cities, influenced by the Greeks, are in the south. Rustic people who tend to be quarrelsome, exasperating yet lovable in their own way, live in the northern region. The proud, independent aristocracy in Galatia are descendants of the Gauls. They remain faithful to their Celtic religion and speak their own language. We are seeing a change in religious preferences. Many of our people have an inclination to follow oriental religions, and they demand more ritualistic sacrifices. Of course, the cult of Apollo is still popular.

On my last trip to Ephesus, I learned that the citizens of Rome are angry at Nero for burning the city. To turn the attention away from himself, Nero has blamed the Christians for the conflagration. They are handy scapegoats because they talk a lot about the world ending in flames. Travelers from Rome report that many Christians, covered with skins of wild animals, have been thrown into arenas, where dogs torment them to death. No doubt the provincial rulers will imitate Rome's example of persecuting Christians. We must keep up with the times, you understand. Welcome to Galatia.

I *am Secundus*, a slave in the home of Marcus, the proconsul. Since being reappointed several times and having his name inscribed on a special coin, Marcus has become very pretentious. We slaves in his household suffer abuse.

Some citizens from Galatia toured Ephesus a few years ago. For several hours each day, they listened to a speaker named Paul. These people accepted Christ and came home determined to begin a church in our town. I went to their Christian service, heard about freedom in Christ, and accepted Him as my Saviour. I am free in my heart, but the life of a slave is difficult. Welcome to Galatia.

I *am Abel*, a Jew who moved from Jericho to Cappadocia for business reasons. Cappadocia is the easternmost point in the entire Roman empire, which is our claim to fame. Efforts to urbanize the province have not been successful. Most of our people live in small communities. Our culture is varied; interior villages tend to display an oriental influence, while the few cities on the coast enjoy the amenities of the Greek-Roman influence.

Our timber resources are found in pine, oak, and fir forests. You probably have heard about the fire in Rome and the consequent rebuilding projects. Since Nero demands more and more wood, the lumber business is booming. Fertilized by lava dust, our pasture land is the best in Asia Minor. I own a stable and breed race horses for the Roman circus. Nearby, at another stable, my neighbor oversees the care of Nero's stud horses.

Severe winters limit agriculture to the growing of hardy, fine quality wheat. Our major export is a fabric made from the hair of goats that roam close to one of the Cilician Gates in the Taurus Mountain range. This tough fabric is used in making tents. The "gates" through which trade and military routes run are actually natural passes in the mountain. Traders daily cross the pass toward Ephesus with supplies of quartz, salt, and silver.

Devotees to our many gods worship at various pagan temples. In the city of Comana, the goddess MA is served by 6,000 priestess. In Venasa, Zeus is worshiped by more than 3,000 folks.

Some Jews in our synagogue traveled in a caravan to Jerusalem for the Feast of Pentecost. After hearing Peter preach, they trusted Jesus and came home actually transformed in their speech and behavior. Because of their witness, I received Jesus into my heart. Now my neighbors ostracize my family because, as they say, we have joined a despised sect. They call us the third race, meaning the Romans are first, the Jews second. Former friends slander my good name and are moving their horses to other stables. My children endure taunts such as, "Evil doers! Evil doers!" Life is difficult. Welcome to Cappadocia.

*I am Titus*, a native of Asia. Though some of the most illustrious cities in the world such as Pergamum, Smyrna, and Ephesus are located closer to the coast, I live in the interior of the province. An interesting bit of trivia that distinguishes us from the other provinces is that Attalus III of Pergamum willed this area to the Senate and the Roman people in 133 BC.

I own one of the many vineyards found here. Our wines are renowned all over Asia Minor. On our rich land, farmers cultivate grain, fruit, and nuts. We mine lead and cut fine marble. Also in the mountains is a supply of unusual building stone that Nero is using to rebuild Rome after the disastrous fire.

Many people worship the Greek and Roman deities, especially the goddess Diana. Emperor worship flourishes. My brother Severus is a Christian serving in the Roman army. His refusal to worship Mithra, the special deity of soldiers, has caused a major conflict with his superiors.

Some Jews in the area traveled to Jerusalem for one of their famous feasts. They returned with the good news that the Messiah had come. My family and many others in this province accepted Christ as Saviour. We worship in my home. Naturally we stopped the orgies, drunkenness, and disgusting idol worship. Now our heathen friends harass and insult us for refusing to join in the pagan festivals. The rumor is that the government might confiscate the property of Christians. My livelihood is at stake.

A chill ran through the Christian community today. The courier posted the news sheet: "Hear Ye! Hear Ye! Human Torches Light Nero's Garden . . . rolling Christians in pitch . . . setting them ablaze . . ." Welcome to Asia.

*I am Levi*, a Jew. Sennacherib deported my ancestors to Babylon. They opted to remain there when many Jews returned to their homeland. My branch of the family migrated to this region, which later became known as Bithynia. Located on the Black Sea, Bithynia has an excellent harbor that I use to export timber. My lumber business is thriving. Since Nero burned most of Rome, he buys all of the oak, beech, chestnut, and walnut I can log. Our marble quarries work 24-hour shifts to meet Nero's demands.

Bithynia is a nice place to live and raise a family. The mountain ranges, running parallel to the coast, leave space for grain fields, and a variety of fruit orchards and pastures. My family and I have joined the Christian church after hearing the messages of itinerant apostles and evangelists. Protected by the Roman assumption that we are a part of Judaism, Christians witness and gain many converts in our province. Lately, because Nero accused Christians of incendiarism, we are under suspicion. The occasional repressions cause anxiety; we wonder when and if severe persecutions will strike. The terrifying news from Rome is that many Christians have been crucified upside down. Welcome to Bithynia.

## An Encouraging Letter Arrives
The Roman government instituted a first class postal system to assist in dispatching edicts to all the cities and provinces. Usually couriers followed a prescribed circuit, dispensing information to cities on a network of roads.

Businesses and private citizens took advantage of these good roads to communicate to people in the provinces. Hired runners or pony riders delivered scrolls along the circuits.

One morning a man—perhaps his name was Silas—debarked at the port of Sinope in Pontus. In his hand he held a letter written by Peter. He left a copy with the Christians in Sinope, instructing them to circulate it throughout Pontus. Then the messenger walked south to Galatia; traveled southeast to western Cappadocia; moved westward, crossing a main trade route to Ephesus before entering the interior of Asia; then on to the last stop, Bithynia. In each province he left a copy of the letter with instructions that it was to be shared. From Bithynia he sailed back to Rome, thus completing a postal circuit.

The word spread throughout the provinces:

"A letter from Peter has come!"

"An epistle from Cephas has arrived!"

I imagine that as the letters circulated, the same scene occurred repeatedly in each province. Christians, buffeted by unalterable circumstances, hovered excitedly over and around the elder who read, "To God's chosen people who live as refugees . . . it may now be necessary for you to be sad for awhile because of the many kinds of trials you suffer."

The reader continued, "Friends, you can endure the mockery and sneers of neighbors. Peter says to follow Christ's example. Let your conduct deny their accusations. Explain to them your hope with gentleness and respect, and be happy if you are insulted because you are Christ's followers.

"To you women married to heathen husbands, Peter says to witness to them through pure and reverent conduct. Friends who are tempted to return to your old life, Peter reminds you that your faith and hope is fixed on God.

"Friends who are slaves, Peter says for you to submit yourselves to your masters and show them complete respect, not only to those who are kind and considerate, but also to those who are harsh. God will bless you for this, if you endure the pain of undeserved suffering because you are conscious of His will."

Those eager listeners surely nodded in earnest approval as the readers continued: "When you face trials, Peter says to look beyond the present crises to life eternal. Trust God to make you stronger because of the trials, and look forward to winning the praise of Jesus. When we suffer for doing good, we are to pay back with a blessing, not be afraid, and not worry. Peter also reminds us to be sure that our suffering is for Christ's sake, not because we murder, steal, or meddle in others' affairs.

"God wants us to silence the ignorant talk of foolish people by the good things we do. We must remember this when we are slandered.

"Persecution is everywhere. Peter asks us to be firm in our faith and resist the devil, because we know that our fellow believers in all parts of the world are going through the same kind of suffering.

"Respect everyone, love your fellow believers, have reverence for God . . . and . . ." The reader hesitated, looked into the wondering eyes of the listeners, then completed the reading by adding, "and respect the emperor. Peter says that for Jesus' sake we can submit ourselves to every human authority." (Based on 1 Peter 1-5.)

I imagine the Christians in the provinces of Asia Minor left those meetings "rejoic[ing] with a great and glorious joy which words cannot express" (1:8*b* TEV). Peter's letter even heightened their self-esteem as he encouraged them to be the "chosen race" (2:9) God had called them to be.

With renewed hope, and with assurance that Jesus understood their suffering, the Christians adjourned their meetings "to follow in His steps" (2:21).

# Asia Minor: The Christian Church

In the Roman world, wealthy landowners hired stewards to manage their property or estates. The steward owned nothing, but was responsible for distributing food and wages to other workers. Using his master's possessions, the steward blessed others. At the owner's request, the steward gave an account of the distribution. As we minister to others with gifts God entrusted to us, we dispense His goodness, not our own. As managers of God's gifts of grace, we must give an account someday.

Christians in Asia Minor lived in tense and dangerous situations. One way to relieve stress of personal discouragement is by helping another person. Peter reminded the Christians that they possessed manifold gifts to benefit each other. *Manifold* means "many colored" and indicates a variety of pleasing ministries. Each member was necessary, because what one member could not do another member was able to do. Variegated ministries complement and support each other.

When I travel, I look forward to night flights. As the plane lifts higher and farther away from the terminal, the darkness resembles a black tarpaulin covering familiar and friendly turf. Then, in a blink of an eye, the countryside winks with intermittent dots of light, a town twinkles, and cities become incandescent clusters. Out in the uncertain gloom of Asia Minor the Christians, ministering with manifold gifts, glowed like diadems in a crown of thorns. They became twinkling lights in the darkness of their world.

Even though Peter expected the Lord's immediate return, he urged the Christians to whom he wrote to continue ministering through their gifts. Elders, either by their position or age, led the simple organization of the church-es. As He had done in Corinth, Rome, and Ephesus, God gave believers every gift necessary to minister and witness in the provinces.

The inns along the Roman roads were filthy and dangerous. Sharing food, shelter, and friendship was practiced so generously that impostors took advantage of Christians who had the gift of hospitality. Christians carried identification credentials in order to protect hospitable people from criminals. Hospitality also meant sharing information, helping travelers transact business, or finding employment for new residents.

The gift of hospitality helped extend Christianity throughout Asia Minor. Believers opened their homes to the apostles, evangelists, prophets, and letter couriers. Paul mentions occasions in his ministry when hospitable members invited the church to meet in their homes (see Rom. 6:15; 1 Cor. 16:19; Col. 4:15). John warned hospitable members not to receive false teachers into their homes, for giving food and lodging would support them in spreading error and evil (see 1 John 10:11). If for some reason guests inconvenienced the hosts, they should continue to share without complaint or mumbling.

People living in perilous circumstances needed to hear a word from the Lord, not a novel ditty from a passing philosopher. Gifted preachers spoke with the authority of a person who received a revelation from God. The gift made the preacher authentic and effective. Peter may have used the words *speaking* or *preaching* as umbrella terms for any or all of the speaking gifts.

Gifted servers lent a helping hand to allow the apostles, pastor/teachers, evangelists, and prophets to exercise their gifts. Helpers also served other members, usually with a one-on-one ministry. I like to define helpers as "the glorious company of stretcher bearers," as seen in Mark 2:1-5.

Helpers accomplish tedious tasks without becoming bored. They know their gifts for doing good are trusts from God. Peter's reminder to "serve with the strength that God gives" is applicable to all the gifts. While each of us is required to use our gifts within our ability, God does not expect ministry beyond our ability. Sometimes presumptuously, we stretch beyond the strength the Lord gives us. Shifting into human overdrive, we dabble with every other gift as well as our own, or with the exception of our own. Then, frustrated, we labor to keep an organization afloat. God, working through our gifts with His power, moves His organism, the church, forward.

Showing hospitality, speaking, and serving is praise to God. Using our gifts, we edify the body and honor God "to Whom belong glory and power forever and ever. Amen" (1 Peter 4:11*b* TEV).

## Followers Pray

Before we leave home on an extended trip, I "close down" the house by unplugging appliances, constantly checking the iron, eating all the leftovers, and canceling the newspaper. Anticipating the journey interrupts our normal routine. Those few hours before departure, living in the house becomes secondary to the journey.

Looking forward to the return of Jesus, many people "close down" ordinary activities and wait. Just today I read in our newspaper that a religious movement predicts the end will be today. In preparation for the end, followers of the movement sold property and homes, quit jobs, left families, and endured abortions. According to the report, if "doomsday" does not occur today, many disappointed people will commit suicide.

The context of Peter's gift passage relates to the belief in Christ's imminent return. However, Peter urged the believers to work while they waited. Their work included praying, loving, and ministering.

Previously we discussed the Holy Spirit's illumination of our minds as well as our emotions. This truth is illustrated in 1 Peter 4:7. Manifold attitudes affect our ability to pray. However, in the text, Peter considers only two possibilities: be self controlled and be alert.

A self-controlled or sober person behaves sensibly instead of wavering between zealousness and indifference. In times of stress, difficult situations, even persecutions, self-control helps a person avoid hysteria. Still joyful, a sober person has an intelligent, responsible approach to life and to prayer. The mind concentrates on deep yearnings, not on trifles. Life's distractions do not interrupt the prayers of a self-controlled person who remains focused.

An alert or watchful person recognizes threats to self and to the body. A vigilant pray-er, he or she has a keen sensitivity to specific needs. The alert person lives in anticipation and expectancy of "possessing the rich blessings that God keeps for his people" (1 Peter 1:4a TEV). Self-control and alertness enable us to pray as we follow in His steps.

Peter gives one further description of followers: they love. Peter described active love as exerting and stretching itself to the limit of endurance, much like a runner who is set on winning a race. Love demands our earnest, most strenuous effort. *Earnest* means "undiluted"; earnest love cannot be weakened. We apply it full strength to the hard-to-love, to those who harass, to those who would take our lives. Earnest love is difficult, isn't it? Earnest love makes us gentle with the weaknesses in other people. Earnest love hides faults and patiently suffers the unkindness of others.

Good managers, praising and loving, also "follow in His steps."

## Welcome to Your Church

Consider members in your church who exercise the three gifts mentioned in the 1 Peter passage. Again, affirm them by placing their names in the appropriate blank. Answering the questions which follow the situations will help you discover your gift if it is listed.

• *Hospitality:* Members of the body with the gift of hospitality may prefer having guests to being alone. Happiness for them is being surrounded by people. They welcome guests into the house "as it is," with no apology for any disarray. Members gifted with hospitality place the comfort of guests as high priority.

Jo issued me a two-fold invitation: to lead a retreat, and to stay in her home. The phone conversation revealed Jo's cheerful disposition, love for people, and desire to share her home. Her plans fell apart. Because of an unexpected situation, Jo gave me directions to a motel. When I stepped into the room, hospitality greeted me, not as a person but as evidence of Jo's gift of hospitality: potpourri in a shell, a delicate fern in a frilly wicker basket, a fruit tray, quarters to use in the refreshment area, two newspapers, and bubble bath. On a bed tray lay a linen napkin with this note pinned to it: "Room service will deliver your breakfast in the morning. Enjoy breakfast in bed. Love, Jo." I felt like a queen. Jo's gift of hospitality overflowed to make a motel room a little bit of home.

Without mumbling or complaining, members with the gift of hospitality open their homes for Bible studies or for mission churches.

I affirm _____'s gift of hospitality.

Do you enjoy making strangers and friends comfortable in your home?

Do you bring people in need into your home without feeling they are an intrusion on your privacy?

Is your house a place where people often come to relax?

• *Preaching:* Some say that people with the speaking gifts "talk too much," for gifted speakers often feel compelled to talk. The many words of gifted speakers comfort, guide, encourage, and warn. Their messages may be directed to individuals or to a congregation. The Holy Spirit addresses the hearers through the preaching, and preaching may include any of the speaking gifts.

I affirm _____'s gift of preaching.

I affirm _____'s speaking gift.
Do you enjoy political involvement?
Are you sensitive to national or international social issues?
Do you express your concern by becoming involved in activities intended to alleviate the problems? For example, your concern about pollution could lead to involvement in an environmental project. Using your gift encourages others to help, also.

• *Service:* Members with the gift of service have a variety of abilities to offer. Without realizing a ministry was performed, other church members benefit from the results of the helper's vital ministry. The church relies on gifted servers to control the sound and light systems, maintain the facilities, trim shrubs, volunteer to check out skates at the Family Life Center, and build risers for choirs.

Chancery Judge Anthony Farese is my neighbor. During the week he travels, administering justice in several counties. The community and the church see his role as a Sunday School teacher, a choir member, and a deacon. From my kitchen window, I see him in the role of a helper.

At 8:00 and again at 9:00 on Sunday mornings, Judge Tony rings the church bell 100 times alerting those in earshot, "Do not forsake the assembling of yourselves together." Between 8:00 and 9:00, depending on the season, Judge Tony sweeps debris from the outside corridors and steps, or scraps ice and shovels snow in an occasional "hard winter." He picks up litter thrown out of vehicles that pass the busy corner. His care makes the church entrances attractive and safe.

I have watched Judge Tony work in the court and in his chamber; I can testify that he helps people in crisis circumstances. I have seen him with a broom on Sunday mornings, and will testify that Judge Tony's gift of service strengthens me.

I affirm _____'s gift of service.

What tasks in your church could not be accomplished without helpers? Which of these do you enjoy doing?

Whether or not service is your gift, what areas of your life need changing to give you more of a servant attitude?

# Gifts: Meeting Needs

"I don't think gifts would work in our church. Chief executive officers of several companies are members. They like to boss so we let them. Most of our members are in high visibility professions—the movers and shakers in our city. Everyone seems to be analytical thinkers." As she expressed a negative opinion about the use of gifts, my friend described the composition of her local church.

Churches have personalities. My husband has been a staff person in four different churches. Each congregation has reflected the qualities and attitudes of the town or area of the city. The reason is simple: people in the community are the people in the church.

## Gifts: Meeting Needs in the Church

The Corinthians' excitable qualities were mirrored in their church. Their enthusiastic worship experience is recorded in 1 Corinthians 14. No doubt, the Romans' seriousness colored their worship. The listing of their gift categories indicate a bent toward organization. The Ephesians' immaturity prompted the need for sound preaching and instruction in doctrine. The Christians' persecution in Asia Minor frustrated their attempts to live their faith. They needed the fellowship of one another.

God designed the physical body with certain needs. We are whole physically, mentally, and emotionally when the needs are satisfied. In like manner, God designed His spiritual body with certain needs. The Holy Spirit assigns gifts to meet the needs in your church. The gifts "work" in every personality-type church.

Follow me to the daily news sheet to learn how the speaking and serving gifts fulfill needs in a local church.

107

# Hear Ye! Hear Ye!

## Speaking Gifts

Need: *An atmosphere in which people can hear God's call*
Gift: *Apostolic*

In a broad sense, *apostle* refers to those commissioned or accredited by the church as Christ's messengers. Missionaries who cross cultures and plant churches demonstrate the apostolic urgency to share the gospel.

Need: *Preaching God's Word*
Gift: *Prophecy*

Holy Spirit-inspired preachers who proclaim biblical principles and truths demonstrate this gift. Prophets warn us to measure our behavior on biblical standards rather than society's standards. The prophet, by writing or speaking, enables Christians to grow spiritually. Lay persons or preachers who urge the application of God's Word to social and moral issues use the gift.

Need: *Instruction*
Gift: *Teaching*

Gifted teachers like to study the Scriptures and share the results of their study with others in an interesting way. They arouse students out of apathy. Teachers clearly communicate biblical truths, causing listeners to say, "I see! I understand."

Need: *Reaching the lost*
Gift: *Evangelism*

In addition to filling the office of an evangelist, people who are constantly burdened for the lost and who have an urgent desire to share their faith possess this gift. Gifted persons enjoy door-to-door evangelistic visitation. They distribute gospel tracts, consistently witness in their lifestyle, and feel comfortable sharing their faith without first cultivating relationships.

Need: *Encouragement*
Gift: *Exhortation*
   The exhorter stimulates others to act on the truth of God's Word. The exhorter is an encourager, comforter, listener, counselor, and guide. The gift is exercised primarily through one-on-one encounters.

Need: *Information*
Gift: *Knowledge*
   This gift stresses the importance of intellect. Paul's ministry emphasized the gift of knowledge. For two years, he debated daily in the hall of Tyrannus in Ephesus. Some manuscripts add that he spoke five hours a day. A result of Paul's sharing knowledge was that "all they which dwelt in Asia heard the word of the Lord Jesus" (Acts 19:10b KJV).
   Biblical researchers, translators of Scriptures, and scholars who share their thoughts in books and material resources exercise the gift. They assist speakers by providing content. Also, members who like to probe the Scriptures for deeper insights have the gift.

Need: *Relate knowledge to life*
Gift: *Wisdom*
   Members with this gift apply knowledge or information to daily experiences. In a complex situation, they distinguish between right and wrong. Those with the gift of wisdom resolve dilemmas by quoting a Scripture or by giving advice. Wisdom enables the person to perceive a weak spot in another's ministry then, with love, give sound advice, pray with, and listen to the other person. According to James 3:15-18, the gift is used with gentleness.

## Serving Gifts
Need: *Support*
Gift: *Helps* or *Serving*

The gift offers a variety of practical ways to help and encourage spiritual growth in church leaders and members. People with the gift of helps enjoy working behind the scenes. They like to usher, cook, decorate tables or bulletin boards, arrange flowers, serve in the kitchen, prepare handwork, collect egg cartons for crafts, drive the van for groups, and volunteer to do menial jobs at the church.

Need: *Fellowship*
Gift: *Hospitality*
     People who enjoy sharing their homes with those in need of food or lodging have the gift. The need may be overnight accommodations for members of a traveling youth choir or a dinner invitation to a lonely friend. The person with this gift expresses the attitude, "What's mine, is your's."

Need: *Financial support*
Gift: *Giving*
     Gifted givers like to take care of the physical needs of others. Often the people who are helped never know who the benefactor is. Gifted givers never grumble about special offerings; they look forward to every opportunity to give. They do not attempt to control the church because of their financial position. However, the gift is not reserved for the wealthy. Gifted givers share from abundant or meager material resources. They give with such cheerfulness that others are blessed.

Need: *Direction*
Gift: *Government, Administration, Leading*
     Gifted leaders administer programs, organize church wide projects, identify and use the gifts of others by delegating. An extroverted personality or the ability to speak publicly are not prerequisites for the gifted leader. Quiet, reserved organizers may possess the gift. Although their demanding work is not always appreciated, the gifted leader expresses spiritual authority with tact and humility.

Need: *Doing kind deeds*
Gift: *Mercy*

A person with the gift of mercy has sensitivity to comprehend the loneliness, despair, and burdens of the underprivileged, the outcasts, and the handicapped. This gift gives the ability to help the people described in Matthew 25:34-46: the hungry, strangers, the sick, prisoners, the naked. The merciful see something good in persons whose actions are anti-social. They can administer tough love. The merciful comfort with a word, a touch, a listening ear. Since their presence is an encouragement, often the spirit of the helper is more of a blessing than the actual aid.

Need: *Power*
Gift: *Faith*

Members who rally the fainthearted possess this gift. They lead in planning for future programs and facilities. When the church faces obstacles, they tend to ignore people who say, "Let's use common sense." Those with the gift of faith trust God's promises and depend on His power.

Need: *Protection*
Gift: *Discernment*

Discerners detect deficiency in the truth of a sermon, a book, a speech, or a conversation. They spot phonies who propagate half-truths. The gift enables a discerner to discriminate between the divine, the human, or the satanic in behavior or in a speech that claims to be from God.

The Holy Spirit endows each believer with at least one of the speaking or serving gifts to meet the needs of the congregation, and to build up the body of Christ. Some believers may have a mixture of gifts, but no one has all the gifts.

The absence of a gift does not excuse a believer from obeying the imperatives or principles that cover most gifts. The exceptions to this are the signifying gifts of tongue-speaking, interpretation, miracles, and healing. No one should say:

"Since I'm not a gifted giver, I'll let those who are gifted pay the preacher and the light bill."

"Since I do not have the gift of evangelism, I'll let my actions show I'm a Christian."

Step up to the posted news sheet for a response to your excuses.

## Hear Ye! Hear Ye!
## Some Examples in Your Church

| A few gifted members | All members |
| --- | --- |
| Prophecy | Should follow the example of the dispersed Christians who went everywhere preaching the Word (see Acts 8:4) |
| Give | Should have the attitude of the giver (see 2 Cor. 6:6-12) |
| Evangelize | Should obey Jesus' words, "You shall be My witnesses" (see Acts 1:8) |
| Possess knowledge | Should grow in the knowledge of God (see Col. 1:10) |
| Show mercy | Should follow the example of the good Samaritan (see Luke10:30-37) |
| Discern | Should "put all things to the test [and] keep what is good" (see 1 Thess. 5:21) |

From time to time, perhaps daily, we will exhibit characteristics of all the gifts. However, we are more comfortable in ministries rooted in our particular gift. Ministries initiated from our own gifts are more effective and lessen the possibility of burn-out.

# Gifts: Meeting Needs in the Community

The shout "Caesar is Lord" stopped. The clamor "Great is Diana of Ephesus" ceased. However, the life-styles represented by those carnal chants echo through the streets of our communities even today.

Follow me again to the daily news sheet. Is the listing on the sheet an adequate description of Corinth? Rome? Ephesus? Your community? My town?

## Hear Ye! Hear Ye!

- People value idleness.

- Dishonest officials cheat.

- Interest rates are high.

- Citizens do not vote.

- Farmers face bankruptcy.

- Eating gets much attention.

- Government handouts deaden initiative and the work ethic.

- Families are dysfunctional.

- Many people live in poverty.

- People seek new gods.

- Unemployment is high.

- Astrologers are trusted.

- Illicit sex is rampant.

- Lewd entertainment is tolerated.

- Sports fans overflow stadiums and idolize excessively-salaried athletes.

The same gifts that enabled the first century churches to survive and thrive in a pagan society are available to us today. I recently read an alarming commentary by a respected columnist stating that decent people will have to "put up" with immorality because of the law of supply and demand. The columnist made an ominous observation that decent people will not be able to change the "cultural tastes" of Americans or the "economic appetite of the entertainment industry."

God energizes His body, the church, with His power: "And how very great is his power at work in us who believe. This power working in us is the same as the mighty strength which he used when he raised Christ from death and seated Him at His right side in the heavenly world . . . God put all things under Christ's feet and gave him to the church as supreme Lord over all things. The church is Christ's body" (Eph.1:19-20,22-23*a* TEV).

The empowered body does not move *en mass.* We circulate separately through our communities, where the Holy Spirit nudges us into ministries rooted in our gifts. Sue babysits so her neighbor can shop or rest. Lea buys crates of citrus fruit and divides it among shut-ins. Mary cares for the pets of her vacationing neighbor. Lucille stocks the hospital's intensive care waiting room with small pillows and hygiene supplies. Rick helps his farmer neighbor bale hay. Laura invites neighbors to a Christmas party. Pat holds a home Bible study in her neighborhood. Our unique gifts become evangelism resources, opening opportunities for us to share our faith and to change our society by leading lost people to confess, "Jesus, Lord."

# *My Gift Is . . .*

Evidently Christians in the first century immediately recognized the Holy Spirit's presence with them, and His gift in them. They allowed Him the freedom to work through them. Therefore, Paul did not list directions for discovering our gifts. However, other peoples' experiences in discovering gifts can guide us.

The golden milestone stood in the center of the Roman Forum. Roads, originating at the marker, linked Rome with every city in the empire. At each mile along the road, smaller versions of the milestone directed travelers to their destinations.

Step up to the golden milestone labeled *prayer*. Examine the methods of gift discovery that radiate from the prayer milestone.

| | PRAYER | |
|---|---|---|
| Accept Others' Affirmation | | Investigate Possibilities |
| Enjoyment Results From Ministry | | Consider Desires |
| Be Available | | Consider Needs |
| Participate in a Variety of Ministries | | Do This. You Can! |

All the methods we use in His kingdom must originate in prayer. Christ as the Head of the body desires members of the body to know their purpose. Ask Him!

James 4:3 admonishes us to examine our motives when we pray. In regard to gifts, negative motives might include a desire to receive praise or status, or to satisfy curiosity about our own gifts as we observe others serving through their gifts. To minister and contribute to church growth are positive motives.

## Methods of Discovery

People use various methods to discover their gifts. You might identify yours in one or more of the following ways:

• *Investigate the possibilities.* Review the gifts in this book. Researching the study enriched my life. However, for every word I have written, hundreds are left unwritten. To increase your own understanding, study commentaries and other resources on spiritual gifts.

• *Consider your desires or inclinations.* What do you like to do? We gravitate toward areas of interest. In fact, some people use their gifts naturally and fail to recognize that much activity originates with the expression of gifts. Feeling good about yourself and enjoying a ministry does not conflict with pleasing God. When we like what we do, others sense our positive motivation, which enhances our ministry.

I suggest a word of caution in regard to desiring gifts. Simply wanting a gift does not assure its possession. The Holy Spirit is the Gift Giver. More often than not our desires mesh with His. First Corinthians 12:31 commands us to desire greater gifts. The verb tense indicates that this command pertains to the whole church. All gifts are necessary for the operation of the body. However, Paul urges the entire church to emphasize the gifts that speak out the message of salvation.

• *Consider the needs of others.* Think about your church and community. What needs or problems concern you? Do you see the hungry, and think of ways to distribute food? Do it! A recent girl's mission organization study session explained how some restaurants donate food to hunger banks and rescue missions. Alice, a girl in our church, liked the idea. She wanted to ask our local restaurants to give left-over food to the hungry in our community. Her interest is a flame that her leader must fan. The concern eventually might define Alice's gift.

Do you notice high grass, snow on the walk, or loose shingles at the home of an elderly person? Mow the lawn, shovel the snow, repair the shingles! What needs often surface in your prayers? A deacon, who consistently prayed for the lonely and shut-ins, now enjoys a ministry with the homebound department.

• *Participate in a variety of experiences.* Step out of your comfort zone. Help prepare and serve a fellowship meal. Teach a Vacation Bible School class. Assist with a missions organization. Visit the jail, nursing home, or hospital. Share your faith in evangelistic visitation. Volunteer to research illustrations for the pastor's sermons, or for a Sunday School teacher. Keep the congregation apprised of the legislature's agenda. Participation in a variety of ministries will help you eliminate those in which you feel uncomfortable or ill-at-ease.

• *Be available and willing to take risks.* Refrain from the tendency to disregard a gift because of its name. For example, *prophecy* sounds theological or pastoral, but laypersons minister through the gift, also. Take advantage of every opportunity to serve. When someone asks for your help, that person may be God's channel directing you toward a gift.

After a nine month in-depth study of juvenile delinquency, our Christian book club asked me to secure a list of initials of a few delinquents so we could pray for them. Early on Monday morning, I sat down in the office of the chief probation officer. Almost immediately pandemonium broke loose. I witnessed several confrontations between teenagers, parents, and police officers. The stage curtains lifted, presenting a panorama of problems that had been hidden from my sheltered life.

Sometime later the probation officer returned to me and apologized saying, "The interruptions made me forget why you came today."

Overwhelmed and embarrassed by the real-life crises, I stammered, "I came for a list of juvenile delinquents' initials. A group of us want to pray for them."

The probation officer's question was tantamount to a call. "Mrs. Calvert, have you ever thought about doing something after you have prayed?"

The need and the gift collided in the office of the probation officer. He offered an opportunity for me to train to become a Volunteer in Probation with the court. Completion of the course was the beginning of my personal long-term mission action activity using my gift of mercy.

One morning my probationer failed to appear at her court hearing. While the police searched for her, I wandered up to the office of my friend who is a state missions leader. In response to her query about my presence, I explained about the book study, the members' desire to pray, and my eventual personal involvement with court. The woman asked me to write the experience so she could use it to promote the book club. I replied, "No way. I don't even write letters."

Almost two years passed. One day I had an overwhelming urge to write the experience for my friend. She mailed the article to the editor of *Royal Service* magazine. In the ensuing years, gifted editors have goaded, stimulated, and advised, but never given up on me. I thank my friend.  Because of her request, she became God's channel, directing my gift of mercy into yet another ministry.

My advice is, "Do what people ask you to do!"

• *Talk with gifted people about gift-discovery.* Carol Noffsinger discovered her gift through practical experiences and by following her natural inclination. Relying on her pup Penny and her ingenuity Carol, an only child, created her own adventures. Enjoying time alone, she became independent. The daughter of a deacon and a Sunday

School teacher, Carol participated in all the church activities. Her mother's influence and Carol's abilities combined to display leadership qualities at an early age. Her gift of leadership is not contrary to her basic nature.

Markers along the way affirmed her leadership gift. On a short term missions assignment in Liberia, West Africa, Carol's missionary supervisors affirmed her ability to direct youth activities with minimal assistance from them. As youth missions director in Georgia, Carol planned, coordinated, and led youth programs. Later in Kentucky, Carol found the planning of retreats, meetings, leadership conferences, and seminars more fulfilling for her than actually doing the event.

Today, as consultant for a missions organization in Kentucky, Carol applies her gifts of leadership to office administration. She plans projects, deals with report forms, trains writers for assignments, and edits. She delegates with ease and shares leadership without being threatened. Carol motivates others not by "swinging off chandeliers with enthusiasm," but in quiet ways.

How did Carol discover her gift? "Leadership and organization are areas where I feel comfortable, and would rather work. I think I'm good at these things, and other people affirm me. I feel good about myself when I accomplish some project or program where I've led and administered."

Why does planning fuel Carol's leadership energy? People benefit. Carol states, "To know, after something is over, that it was a success because of what people tell you and how it changes their lives . . . was and is what makes my job worth doing."

• *Enjoyment, excitement, and satisfaction result from ministry.* Ministries exercised through your gift result in joy and fulfillment, not boredom and frustration. In my 20 plus years of being a court volunteer, I never have said, "Oh, me. Today I have to listen to the trials of Susie and her family." I am always eager to see my probationer friends. I recognize that the Holy Spirit creates that eagerness. He uses me as a channel to minister.

On the other hand, some days I say, "Oh, me. It's rain-ing. Bobbie probably doesn't want company on a rainy day. There will be a better time to talk to her about the Lord." Without the gift of evangelism, I make excuses for not talking to Bobbie even though I know I should.

• *Accept affirmation from others in the body.* Listen to the encouragement and evaluation of other Christians. Accept sincere compliments as expressions of gratitude for how your gift has blessed and ministered to their needs. Affirmation also makes us accountable. If our Christian friends realize and acknowledge our gifts, we feel more responsible in using them in ministry.

As I affirm some of my friends, you may think of those you know whom you want to affirm.

From the rural Tidewater of Suffolk, Virginia through the suburbs and communities between Portsmouth and Newport News, to the fringes of the city of Richmond, and on into Mississippi's Pearl River and Jackson, Dottie Williamson has planted churches. In the process, she touched small town residents and city dwellers, profes-sional folks and farmers, retirees in the open spaces of Pearl River, and residents of all ages in the multi-family apartments of Jackson. Dottie criss-crosses cultures. I affirm her missions zeal as a modern day apostle. Thank you, Dottie.

Believers with the gift of prophecy speak out on issues because they have a keen understanding of the results of certain trends. Those with this gift study, interpret, and proclaim the truth from God's revelation. Dr. Earl Kelly's "thus saith the Lord" messages from the pulpit have helped, encouraged, and comforted me. Dr. Kelly, I affirm your gift. Thank You.

Persons with the gift of teaching help others translate Christian belief into Christian behavior. They share the Scriptures in an interesting, informative manner. Mrs. Street communicated the plan of salvation simply so that I was able to say, "I see my sin." Mrs. Street, I affirm your teaching gift. Thank you.

The exhorter motivates others to action, nurtures another's faith, and ministers to aching hearts. Miss Mary Essie Stephens, I affirm your gift to encourage, guide, and stimulate. Thank you.

The person with the gift of faith has a steadfast confidence that God will overcome any difficulty to accomplish His purpose. Bob, my husband, believed that God wanted a church building on the corner lot. He thanked God in advance and unconditionally looked for an answer. All obstacles vanished and in their place a brick sanctuary now houses the body of Christ. Bob, I affirm your gift of faith. Thank you.

Virginia Cartwright manifested practical compassion (mercy) and hospitality by opening her home to elderly strangers when their house burned. Virginia's sensitivity caused her to become a burden-bearer when she learned of the tragedy. I affirm your gifts, Virginia. Thank You.

The experiences of my friend Barbara Joiner inspire me to pray more specifically, and to give more generously to missions. Her stories weave my emotions like a French braid, or maybe pigtail plaits. She teaches through laughter and through tears. "Pizazzy" state youth missions conventions prove her ability to incorporate the gifts of many people. A variety of missions trips prove her ability to organize toward worthwhile goals, to insist the team members reach and even stretch their potential, and to guide by example. As a result of her leadership gift young ladies involved become flexible and remain unflappable, regardless of the conditions that greet them. Barbara, I affirm your gift mixture. Thank you.

I do not remember his name, but his contribution to my life is indelible. In the heat of summer and the ice of winter, he stood on the corner in front of the bakery where he sometimes sought shelter. Though his furrowed brow indicated urgency, his broad smile expressed joy. His shirt pockets bulged with tracts that explained the plan of salvation. Every passerby received a handshake, a tract, and an invitation. Halting words tumbled from his mouth, "God loves you. Love him back." A birth defect did not deter the Holy Spirit from witnessing through the young man.

One day, word of his death spread through the community. Mourners from all over the city, those whose lives he had touched, packed the sanctuary. Together we celebrated the young man's wholeness in heaven. Many of the mourners loved God because the young man asked them to. My unnamed friend, you inspire me to tell people, "God loves you. Love him back." Thank you.

Roscoe Brannon ministered as an usher. His salesman professionalism was evident in the friendly, relaxed way with which he met those who gathered on Sunday. Roscoe had perfected the usual ushering qualities: a firm handclasp, appropriate greetings, remembering names. However, Roscoe was more than a doorkeeper. He prepared people for worship. His welcome, "Come into the house," echoed a personal conviction of "I was glad when they said to me, 'Let us go to the house of the Lord!'" (Ps. 122:1 RSV).

"Come into the house" meant more than "take a seat." It suggested, "Come into safety, security; come where you can sob over sin; come into forgiveness, acceptance; come where you can sing, shout; come into solace." Between the front door and the pew, seekers became worshipers. Roscoe Brannon helped to make the difference. I affirm his gift.

Jeanette Calvert serves through her sewing talent. Selecting a piece of brocade, a colorful braid, and a jeweled button, she seams together authentic costumes for Christmas and Easter pageants. Her attention to detail and obvious delight in her work enhance the congregation's ability to worship. Jeanette, I affirm your service gift. Thank you.

Mrs. Simpson shared with me her experiences with a tribe of people who had no written language. Patience described this Wycliffe Bible translator's gift. Patience in listening to sounds, writing them phonetically, forming words, then compiling simple primers. Patience in teaching adults to read their own language. Patience in the painstaking process of finding the exact words to translate God's love. The result was hearing a grown man exclaim, "God talks our language!" Mrs. Simpson, I affirm your gift of knowledge. Thank you.

Even after following these markers for discovering your gift, sometimes the Lord impresses your mind with, "Do this. You can!"

These friends remind me that God loves and cares for me enough to provide gifted people to minister to my needs. When we sincerely believe that the Holy Spirit has given a variety of gifts to the church, we will ask, "What gift of mine does God intend to use to strengthen those who strengthen me?" Women have said to me:

"I cannot sing or teach; but I like to visit, plan menus, and be a caring neighbor. I have the gift of helps."

"I recognize that my money should contribute to, not control, the church's finances. I have the gift of giving."

"I empathize with the handicapped. I have the gift of mercy."

"I am consistently asked to lead projects and chair committees. I have the gift of leadership."

"When others say, 'It can't be done,' I expect God to provide a way. I have the gift of faith."

"I like to relate the scriptures to social and moral issues. I have the gift of prophecy."

"People respond to challenges that I present. I have the gift of exhortation."

"People come to me for encouragement. I, too, have the gift of exhortation."

Women who confirm their own gifts have a happy sense of freedom that comes in knowing they are special. Confirming your gift eliminates a low self esteem. An unhealthy self-image with the accompanying feelings of inadequacy and inferiority is a heavy burden to carry through life. Good News! God has graced your unique personality with a unique gift. You are able to minister through your gift in ways not duplicated in any other life. You are competent!

God has appointed you a particular place in His body, the church. Since the Holy Spirit empowers the gift, you will accomplish the purpose that God has in mind. Knowing your gift is mercy, teaching, or helping, you do not consider yourself worthless or competitive because you are not an evangelist, an exhorter, or an administrator. You belong!

God has promised you will never lose your usefulness, "for the gifts and calling of God are without repentance" (Rom. 11:27 KJV). You are secure. Your gift helps you discover who you are: a person of worth!

Women who have a healthy self-esteem occasionally find themselves struggling in a thin fog of pity and self-doubt. Often the reason is that someone spurned, either by action or by word, the ministry for which they are gifted. In reality, every person will not receive our intended ministry. Our gifts do not insulate us from the barbs of life. Corinth, Rome, Ephesus, and Asia Minor prove that fact.

On days when I feel like asking "what's the use?" I read Romans 16. Easily overlooked in a hasty reading of Paul's greetings, I meet two people who encourage me. In the Roman Empire slaves were named by numbers: Primus, Secundus, Tertius, Quartus, and so forth. Gaius, Paul's host in Corinth, owned slaves. His number three slave, Tertius, became a Christian. Because Tertius could read and write, Paul dictated the Roman letter to him.

When Paul completed dictating the "hello's" to friends in Rome, Tertius added, "I, Tertius, the writer of this letter, send you Christian greetings" (16:22). Number four slave, also a believer, stood close by. Perhaps he gave a signal to be included because Paul adds, "Erastus, the city treasurer, and our brother Quartus send you their greetings" (16:23). For any number of reasons you may feel like a Tertius or a Quartus. However, as a member of Christ's body, entrusted with a gift to encourage His other children, *you are Primus!*

# Corinthian Courier

*Calendar of Events*
Today in Corinth: Christians to meet in the home of Titus Justus to continue the reading of a letter from the Apostle Paul. Today's subject: *agape love.*
Tomorrow in Corinth: slave auction. Robust Christian will sell himself to gain funds for the support of fellow believers.

*Mirror sale*
Are your mirrors fading? Do you need a clearer reflection? Corinthian mirrors of highly polished metal are on sale at the Agora across from the Peirene Fountain.

*Christian Jumps onto Burning Pyre*
A Christian voluntarily burned himself to death today in one of the public squares. His act was reminiscent of the Indian fanatic whose public suicide caused an uproar throughout the country several years ago. In an interview prior to his self-sacrifice, Luis shouted, "I want to be a martyr for the cause of Christ."

A pagan Corinthian woman, scanning headlines in the *Corinthian Courier*, might think: "'Burned for a boast' is what we said about that egotistical Indian. He jumped into the flames, saying that old age might lessen his enjoyment of life. These Christians who commit suicide or sell themselves into slavery must be the same kind of egotist . . . *Agape.* A new word for love? Does this sensual city need another kind of love?"
Her reading is interrupted by the clashing cymbals of Cybele's devotees trying to gain the attention of their god-

dess. Clutching a tambourine so she can join the procession, the Corinthian woman glances into the mirror. "My reflection is hazy. Tomorrow I'll buy a new mirror."

Meanwhile, the Corinthian Christians gathered at Titus Justus' home. Their amiable greetings disguise their self-centered thoughts:

"My ecstatic speaking is more rapturous than Phara's."

"My eloquent speeches sway the crowd."

"Regardless of what is discreet in feminine dress, I will not wear a veil. I'm a free woman."

"I hope that heathen judge forces Lucius to pay for my bent chariot."

"That poor Pausias family cannot eat with us at the love feast. I bought only food for our clique . . . oh, I mean, close friends."

"I heard that Mai attended the feast of the god Dionysus. I thought she was sincere about Christianity. I guess she's not."

"This offering will ensure that my name be engraved on the sacrificial givers' plague."

Seated before the congregation, the teacher unrolled the scroll and began to read: "I may be able to speak the languages of men and even of angels, but if I have no love, my speech is no more than a noisy gong or a clanging bell."

Incomparable, dignified, and noble are a few extravagant words used to describe 1 Corinthians 13. Often removed from the list of writings that discuss spiritual gifts, it is appreciated as a pinnacle of love literature. Actually the chapter is the center of a trilogy, connecting Chapter 12, where a variety of gifts are listed, with Chapter 14, which confronts the proper use of gifts. Paul did not intend to write an essay on love. With his infinite vocabulary, he logically proved that love escorts the use of gifts. Musing on the beauty of the passage, we often miss the message.

Again today, I basked in the beautiful simplicity of words that beckon Christians to live a significant life, not just listen to poetic phrases. The exquisite phrases challenge us to step from behind facades, to touch people, to take risks, to swallow pride, to forgive! Paul and Peter wrote about spiritual gifts to people living in Corinth, Rome, Ephesus, and the Provinces of Asia Minor. In each letter, they also discussed the behavior that should accompany the gifts.

Love is never called a spiritual gift. Of course, we recognize that Jesus, God's love personified, is our Gift. We did not merit His sacrifice. We know that the Holy Spirit is our ascension gift who brought us individual gifts. However, the love Paul wrote about is a fruit of the Spirit. It is perhaps all the fruit wrapped in one word—*love*.

Love is the motivating factor in our lives. Love is the absolutely necessary medium for exercising all the gifts. The contrast in Chapter 13 is between using spiritual gifts with love and using spiritual gifts without love. The use of gifts does not assure that love is the motive for their use. The point is that without love the gifts lose their proper effectiveness, value, and reward. To illustrate this, Paul chose several gifts highly prized by the Corinthians and said:

Without love, the most eloquent language, the most impressive speaking, is ineffective. Beautiful words without love are like the unmelodious, repetitious noise of the heathen's cymbals. "Clanging cymbal" and "wailing over the dead" are rooted in the same Greek word. Without love, communication causes sadness. Words hurt. If used for display, the most coveted speaking gifts irritate.

Without love, proclamation of God's revelation, spiritual insights, and comprehension of Biblical truths create an intellectual snobbery, cause contempt for people with less visible gifts, and bore listeners.

Without love, faith that moves a mountain manipulates that mountain right into another's path. Faith absorbed in its own accomplishments produces a domineering attitude.

Without love, many deeds which seem unselfish are

motivated by pride. Without love, even self-sacrifice or selling oneself into slavery is valueless because it seeks the applause of men.

The gifts themselves have spiritual worth. They can function through imperfect lives and enrich others. Paul did not say that without love, the gifts lose their genuineness. Yet if self-interest instead of strengthening other believers is the motive, the possessor of the gift is nothing. The reward is human honor. Even the Lord will refuse to recognize busy activity (see Matt. 7:21-23).

The Corinthian believers gloried in the impressive gifts and sensational services. They learned that three of their most cherished gifts—tongues, prophecy, knowledge—are temporary. Only Christian character abides.

Human life progresses through stages of development. Actions appropriate in childhood are improper for adults. Similarly, our spiritual growth and that of our church is a progressive understanding of God and His ways.

For example, our best knowledge of God is indirect through His creation, through the Scriptures, and even in His clearest revelation, Jesus. Paul used a local metaphor to contrast direct and indirect knowledge. The Corinthians manufactured mirrors of highly polished bronze. At best, the image was blurred. So it is with our comprehension of God. Even through the gift of prophecy, our reflection of God is imperfect.

We are aware of God through the effects of His presence. I watched the foam-tipped waves lap the shore, felt the breeze brush my face. I could not grasp the wind, even though I recognized its presence. Inability to catch the wind did not diminish the pleasant moment on the beach.

The realization that our present knowledge of God is dim does not lessen the beauty of the experiences we have with Him. By developing the gifts even with limited insight, we prepare for greater understanding. One day, when we turn to see God's reflection in the mirror of His creation, or of life's experiences, we will see Him face to face. Within the fellowship of heaven, our fragmentary knowledge will be complete.

*Eros* (sensual love) saturated the Corinthian society. *Agape* love startled the new Christians. Godlike agape love values, manifests generous concern, and is faithful toward others. Agape is a moral, intellectual quality as opposed to senses, instincts, sentiment. Selfless, it seeks the best for others, even enemies. By an act of will, agape love continues to love regardless of the response. New agape love enhanced the believers' fellowship, strengthened their quality of life, and changed their behavior. The Christians understood that their love, not their doctrine, attracted non-believers. Properly used, the gifts tangibly express God's love.

What kind of love should motivate the gifts and control our relationships? Paul did not define an abstract idea. Instead, he featured feelings that are apt to produce clashes among people and described how love would act (see 1 Cor. 13:4-7).

## Love Actions

Actions rooted in love are:

• *patient and kind.* Love tenderly stands the strain of irritating people, goes the second mile to help one who has hurt you, and is never inconsiderate, critical, brusque, or intolerant.

• *never jealous.* Love does not belittle the good qualities or gifts of others and is content with its opportunities, abilities, possessions, and position.

• *never proud.* Love does not advertise emptiness by boasting; does not swagger as a result of its experiences, abilities or position; is teachable and receptive.

• *never rude.* Love is pleasing, courteous, gracious, tactful, mannerly; love is never harsh or blunt.

• *never insisting on its own way.* Love serves, accepts the differences in gifts, does not censure another's relationship with the Lord, and produces gentleness which will not allow itself to hurt others.

• *never irritable.* Love is never touchy or bad-tempered,

sarcastic, or sullen; is angry at injustice and sin, never at personal hurt.

• *never resentful*. Love purifies our reactions to daily, petty frustrations; love does not brood over hurts or memorize injustices, or hold grudges.

• *never rejoicing in wrong, but rejoicing in the right*. Love does not gossip, relish scandal, gloat over the failure or misfortune of another; love provides an atmosphere for people to learn from their mistakes.

Like Jesus, love never gives up, always draws a veil over another's wrong-doing (see Prov. 10:12), and tries to restore and build up. Love desires to bring positive blessing, regardless of whether it is misunderstood or criticized.

Like Jesus, love believes the best as long as it can, then if love is disappointed, it remembers the struggle of the one who failed. Love is not gullible nor cynical; love possesses a calm confidence that God has purpose and reason for the circumstances in our lives. Jesus went to the cross believing that eleven men would continue His mission and spread His message until it reached Corinth, Rome, Ephesus, Asia Minor, and your community.

Like Jesus, love never despairs, because attitude and life perspective are rooted in Jesus. The Galilean community laughed and the fathers balked. However, Jesus saw possibilities in the fishermen and the crusader Saul. Love seeks to transform unlikable, negative, churlish people, because love hopes.

Like Jesus, love continues even when rebuffed. Natural love will not survive without a response. No circumstance can quench agape love. Through hardship and discouragement, it stays under the burden and continues to trust in God's love.

Paul painted a word picture of Jesus. Love is Christ-likeness. Our likeness to Christ is proportionate to our love for others. We are not equally gifted; but agape love, available to all, must be the motivation for those with the most obvious gifts and for those with less obvious ones.

Love, the medium for expressing gifts, is superior to the gifts. Personal relationships and the ministries of our churches could be revolutionized if we allowed agape love to grip us.

Spiritual gifts are temporary. In heaven we will not need each other's ministry. In the here and now, we express love to one another through our gifts. Loving others, we behave like Jesus and we polish quality that we will use eternally. If I said continuously to God, "I love you," I could never repeat the words enough to express the depths of devotion. The only way I can respond to God's love for me is by loving others in practical ways.

She was only fourteen, but Susie had never known a day free from anxiety. I watched her exist through multiple crises. My hope for her was slim. Drained of all emotion, she moaned the latest horrendous incident. I was speechless. After a long silence, I interpreted to God, "Holy Father, Stuart is loving You."

When you minister through your gift of teaching, helping, organizing, showing hospitality or mercy; when you demonstrate faith; when you discern, prophesy, or share your knowledge and wisdom; when you exhort or verbalize your faith; when you give . . . the Holy Spirit interprets to God, "Holy Father, Your child is loving You."

# Study Plan

A study of this book should lead readers to:
•acknowledge the Holy Spirit as the giver of gifts to every believer;
•determine their spiritual gifts;
•accept the gifts as God's method of edifying the church;
•study gift ministries in first century and present day churches.

**Preparation:**
__Encourage all participants to bring their Bibles; have extra Bibles for those who do not bring their own.
__Ask each participant to bring a napkin to the study.
__Enlist four people to help with the study by being prepared to present summary information about people who live in Corinth, Ephesus, Rome, and Asia Minor. Give each person a copy of the book far enough ahead of the study for preparation.
__Enlist two others to present the suggested role play.
__Be thoroughly familiar with contents of this book to help you guide discussions.
__Be prepared to present "tour guide" information about customs and culture of the locations.
__Prepare and duplicate activity materials described throughout the study plan. Materials to be prepared in advance are marked with an asterisk.
__Have pencils and several sheets of paper for all participants.
__Display a map showing New Testament church locations.
__Decorate the room where the study will be held with cardboard "columns" covered with marbleized paper or

similar first century decorations. You might wear clothing typical of that period.

__Encourage those who will attend to read the book before coming.

__Prepare a banner with this statement: *The unity of the body of Christ is not characterized by uniformity but by an exciting diversity of gifted people.*

Following most sections of study suggestions, discussion questions are given. These may be used at appropriate times throughout the study to guide group discussions. At other times, they may be discussed in small groups of two to four participants. Also, writing answers to these questions will meet Church Study Course requirements for personal learning activities.

**Leading the Study:**
1. *On 3-by-5 cards, write the names of body parts that are sometimes overlooked (such as eye lash; thumb nail; little toe; knee cap; shin bone; shoulder blade). As participants arrive, give them a card with these instructions: Talk to others about the importance of your body part. Try to convince them yours is the most important one, and is necessary for the other parts to function.

Ask participants to tell thoughts they had during this activity. (Examples: Did you feel boastful? Were you envious of another person's body part? Did you say things that weren't really true in order to make your part seem more important?) Review Paul's comparison of a physical body to the body of Christ (see pages 42-48 and 1 Cor. 12:12-26). Lead in prayer, thanking God for Christ, the Head of the church's body, and for each member's unique place in the body. Ask participants to look at the banner* and explain what the statement means to them.
(10 minutes)

2. Introduce yourself to participants as their tour guide who will lead them on a tour of some of the cities of the

first century. *Write Ephesus, Corinth, Rome, and Asia Minor on separate sheets of paper; tape them to the wall behind you. Point out the location of each city or area on the map, giving a brief overview of the cultural and economic setting. Be sure to mention the custom of taking left-overs home in a napkin (see page 53). As you arrive at each city, introduce one of the citizens of that city who will tell about some fellow citizens who live there.

This section of the study should be limited to 20 minutes; spend no more than 5 minutes at any one location. As they listen, ask participants to make notes of gifts they perceive that God might have given these people for use in His church. Following the guided tour, remind participants that people like these new Christians were the ones who made up the first church, and to whom Paul and Peter wrote their letters.

To experience what a Corinthian service might have been like, ask all participants to speak at the same time, each telling about how the Lord has worked in their lives. Tell participants that you will throw a ball* to one person; only that person will be silent, and listen to the surrounding noise. Then that person will throw the ball to another, and will again speak. After three minutes, ask participants to share feelings and thoughts they had during this experience.

•How did the pagan beliefs and practices of the first Christians affect the new church?
•Why is it important for there to be some order in a worship service?
•How do you think these new Christians felt about the hostile society's reaction toward them?
•How could their gifts from the Spirit help them face their problems?
•How would self-control, alert prayers, and earnest love help the persecuted Christians? Is the same still true today?
(30 minutes)

3.  Arrange participants into four groups. \*Write the following Scripture references and page numbers on four pieces of paper and give one to each group.
    1.  1 Corinthians 12,14 (pages 19-30)
    2.  Romans 12:1-21 (pages 49-64)
    3.  Ephesians 4:15-32 (pages 75-85)
    4.  1 Peter 4:7-11 (pages 91-102)

Each group is to imagine they are the church or churches to whom Paul or Peter is writing in these passages. As group members study the verses, instruct them to note the gifts that are mentioned. Allow five minutes for groups to work, then five minutes for each group to report, keeping in mind they are reporting as members of the first century church. Each group is to tell the gifts they discovered, and suggest how that gift would be used in their church. Write the gifts on the left side of a chalkboard or large sheet of paper as they are given. Leave room to write on the right side of the board during Step 8.
(25 minutes)

4.  Ask two members to role play two early Christians debating the importance of their own gifts. This might be two of the citizens who were introduced earlier. Guide a group discussion of the role play by asking these questions:

•How can we guard against making one gift measure the spiritual depth of every member?
•Why did Paul consider preaching and teaching the highest gifts?
•How can wrong attitudes about spiritual gifts cause dissention and problems within the church body, instead of accomplishing the purpose for which they were given?
(10 minutes)

5.  During a 15 minute break, serve fruit and nuts. Remind participants they are to follow first century custom, and take some home in the napkins they brought with them.

6. When participants return to the study area, have paper*
in each chair with the words FIRST CENTURY and
(YOUR CITY) written from top to bottom to form an
acrostic. After FIRST CENTURY, ask members to write
words that describe the first century churches. After the
letters of your city, members will write words that
describe your city and/or church. Encourage members to
work with the person next to them. Allow a few minutes
to compare responses in the large group. Ask participants
to rank, on a scale of 1 to 10 (with 1 very different--10 very
much alike) how your city and church compares in some
of these ways with cities and churches of the first century.

•Have present-day churches lost vitality by delegating
responsibility to a professional ministry? Explain your
answer.
•Does today's society influence Christians to seek sensational gifts? Explain your answer.
•How do adults, as well as children, mimic society's life-
styles? How is this reflected in the church?
•What attitudes threaten the use of our gifts?
•How are spiritual gifts sometimes misused? How can we
overcome the obstacle of improper attitudes?
(15 minutes)

7. Tell participants you are now tour guide of (current
year). Ask them to look again at the lists of gifts and think
of ways these gifts are used in the church today. Ask members to contrast use of the gifts today to the first century.
   Ask participants to brainstorm elements that would
make a "perfect" church body, with all members using
their Spirit-given gifts as intended.

•What is the difference in using spiritual gifts with and
without love?
•What would be characteristics of a church body functioning as Christ intended?
•What hinders this from happening, and must be elimi-

nated for the church to function properly? (Responses will include jealousy, greed, misunderstanding.)

•For your church to demonstrate the ideal church's behavior, what changes should you and others make in your understanding and use of gifts?

•How does a biblical perspective on giftedness affect the way we view other believers?

(20 minutes)

8.  Ask participants to list needs in their community, and within their church family. Write responses on the right side of the chalkboard. Next, as members look at the list of gifts, ask them to suggest which gifts God could use to meet those needs. Draw lines from the need to the gift. (Several needs and gifts will overlap.)

•Why is it imperative that the gifts be exercised with love?

•How is exercising the gifts of the Spirit a way of demonstrating Christ's love?

•How does Paul's ministry encourage us never to think someone is beyond God's grace?

•What are the results of our losing our first love?

•How does permanent love contrast with passing gifts?

•What is the reward of those who use their gifts without love?

•How does the Holy Spirit illuminate our minds as well as our emotions?

(15 minutes)

9.  Review the suggestions for ways to discover personal gifts (see pages 115-124). Ask members to reflect on their own interests and abilities as you read aloud the questions on pages 31-33, 65-68, 86-87, 103-105. After you have read the questions allow time for participants to discuss their responses in groups of two to four. Encourage members to affirm these gifts in others, also.

•How does knowing what our gifts are eliminate a low self image?
•Why do we sometimes feel ineffective or discouraged, or experience burn out in ministry?
•How can your spiritual gifts be used as evangelism resources?
•How does being a manager or steward of a gift provide motivation to use it?
•What are characteristics of a good manager?
(10 minutes)

10. As a closing meditation, ask participants to reflect on these questions:

•In what ways will a life sacrificed on an altar alter a Christian's behavior?
•Have my attitudes or actions been divisive in the body of Christ?
•Have I overlooked the importance of my gifts?
•How can I promote unity among believers?

Lead participants in reading 1 Corinthians 13 as a choral reading. Read Ephesians 4:1-7,16 as a closing prayer. (5 minutes)

# The Church Study Course

This book is course number 03:355 in the subject area: Christian Growth and Service. The Church Study Course is a Southern Baptist educational system consisting of short courses for adults and youth combined with a credit and recognition system. Credit is awarded for each course completed. A record of awards will be maintained by the Church Study Course Awards Office. Annually, copies of the credits accumulated will be sent to churches for distribution to members participating in Church Study Course.

The Church Study Course is sponsored by the Sunday School Board, Woman's Missionary Union, the Brotherhood Commission, and other Southern Baptist Convention agencies.

Credit for the course may be obtained in two ways: (1) Conference or class—read the book and participate in a 2 ½ hour study; (2) Individual study—read the book and write responses to all discussion questions in the study plan.

Request credit on Form 725 Church Study Course Enrollment/Credit Request (Revised) available from the Church Study Course Awards Office, Sunday School Board, 127 Ninth Avenue, North, Nashville, TN 37234.

Complete details about the Church Study Course system, courses available, and diplomas offered may be found in a current copy of the Church Study Course Catalog available from the church office or Church Study Course Awards Office.